# Tourism and India

Tourism to and within India has undergone some important changes in recent years, as shown by the rising numbers of international tourists and increase in domestic tourism. This has led to the redevelopment and rebranding of many of its destinations as the Indian government has begun to recognise the potential importance of tourism to the Indian economy and has begun to invest in tourism infrastructure. It is also recognised that as its economy continues to grow at a rapid rate, India will also become one of the most important countries in terms of future outbound tourism.

*Tourism and India* is the first book to specifically focus on and fully analyse the issues facing contemporary India both as a destination and as a potential source of tourists. The book analyses previous research and applies critical theory to key aspects of tourism in India and supports this with a wide range of examples to illustrate the key conceptual points. As such the book examines aspects of tourism in India including tourism governance, cultural tourism, heritage tourism and nature-based tourism from the supply side and international tourism, domestic tourism, outbound tourism and the Indian diaspora from the demand side.

This timely book includes original research to offer insights into India's future development in terms of tourism. It will be of interest to students, researchers and academics in the areas of tourism, geography and related disciplines.

**Kevin Hannam** is Professor of Tourism Development and Director of the Centre for Research into the Experience Economy (CREE) at the University of Sunderland, UK.

**Anya Diekmann** is Assistant Professor and co-director of the research centre Laboratoire Interdisciplinaire Tourisme, Territoires et Sociétés (LIToTeS) at the Université Libre de Bruxelles (ULB), Belgium.

# Contemporary Geographies of Leisure, Tourism and Mobility

Series Editor: C. Michael Hall, Professor at the Department of Management, College of Business and Economics, University of Canterbury, Private Bag 4800, Christchurch, New Zealand

The aim of this series is to explore and communicate the intersections and relationships between leisure, tourism and human mobility within the social sciences.

It will incorporate both traditional and new perspectives on leisure and tourism from contemporary geography, e.g. notions of identity, representation and culture, while also providing for perspectives from cognate areas such as anthropology, cultural studies, gastronomy and food studies, marketing, policy studies and political economy, regional and urban planning, and sociology, within the development of an integrated field of leisure and tourism studies.

Also, increasingly, tourism and leisure are regarded as steps in a continuum of human mobility. Inclusion of mobility in the series offers the prospect to examine the relationship between tourism and migration, the sojourner, educational travel, and second home and retirement travel phenomena.

The series comprises two strands:

**Contemporary Geographies of Leisure, Tourism and Mobility** aims to address the needs of students and academics, and the titles will be published in hardback and paperback. Titles include:

**The Moralisation of Tourism**
Sun, sand . . . and saving the world?
*Jim Butcher*

**The Ethics of Tourism Development**
*Mick Smith and Rosaleen Duffy*

**Tourism in the Caribbean**
Trends, development, prospects
*Edited by David Timothy Duval*

**Qualitative Research in Tourism**
Ontologies, epistemologies and methodologies
*Edited by Jenny Phillimore and Lisa Goodson*

**The Media and the Tourist Imagination**
Converging cultures
*Edited by David Crouch, Rhona Jackson and Felix Thompson*

**Tourism and Global Environmental Change**
Ecological, social, economic and political interrelationships
*Edited by Stefan Gössling and C. Michael Hall*

**Cultural Heritage of Tourism in the Developing World**
*Dallen J. Timothy and Gyan Nyaupane*

**Understanding and Managing Tourism Impacts**
*Michael Hall and Alan Lew*

Forthcoming:

**An Introduction to Visual Research Methods in Tourism**
*Tijana Rakic and Donna Chambers*

**Routledge Studies in Contemporary Geographies of Leisure, Tourism and Mobility** is a forum for innovative new research intended for research students and academics, and the titles will be available in hardback only. Titles include:

1 **Living with Tourism**
   Negotiating identities in a Turkish village
   *Hazel Tucker*

2 **Tourism, Diasporas and Space**
   *Edited by Tim Coles and Dallen J. Timothy*

3 **Tourism and Postcolonialism**
   Contested discourses, identities and representations
   *Edited by C. Michael Hall and Hazel Tucker*

4 **Tourism, Religion and Spiritual Journeys**
   *Edited by Dallen J. Timothy and Daniel H. Olsen*

5 **China's Outbound Tourism**
   *Wolfgang Georg Arlt*

6 **Tourism, Power and Space**
   *Edited by Andrew Church and Tim Coles*

7 **Tourism, Ethnic Diversity and the City**
   *Edited by Jan Rath*

# Tourism and India

A critical introduction

**Kevin Hannam and
Anya Diekmann**

Routledge
Taylor & Francis Group

LONDON AND NEW YORK

First published 2011
by Routledge
2 Park Square, Milton Park, Abingdon, Oxfordshire OX14 4RN

Simultaneously published in the USA and Canada by Routledge
711 Third Avenue, New York, NY 10017

First issued in paperback 2014

*Routledge is an imprint of the Taylor & Francis Group, an informa business*

Typeset in Times New Roman by Prepress Projects Ltd, Perth, UK

*British Library Cataloguing in Publication Data*
A catalogue record for this book is available from the British Library

*Library of Congress Cataloguing in Publication Data*
A catalog record has been requested for this book

ISBN13: 978-1-138-88355-0 (pbk)
ISBN13: 978-0-415-55729-0 (hbk)

For Kieran, Alexander, Alexandra, Felix and Hannah

# Contents

# Figures

# Tables

# Boxes

# Acknowledgements

First of all, we wish to thank our two families (parents, partners, children and siblings) and all of our friends for their support in writing this book. It wouldn't have been possible if they hadn't helped us out during the various trips we have made to India and during the numerous weekends and evenings of writing. Also, we would like to thank our friends and colleagues from both our own and other universities around the world who have helped us not only practically by taking over various tasks, but also through the numerous constructive discussions and exchanges we have had.

Kevin would like to thank his PhD supervisors, Dr Pam Shurmer-Smith and Professor Graham Chapman, for sending him to India back in 1996 ostensibly 'to find something out'. He would like to thank the National Institute for Rural Development (NIRD), Hyderabad, and the Indira Gandhi National Forest Academy (IGNFA) for their kind assistance and hospitality, in particular R. K. Bajpai, who has remained a good friend.

Anya would like to particularly thank her friend Hema Chhatwal who took her to India for the first time and made this first encounter with the country an unforgettably positive and enriching experience, especially because of the warm welcome given by Hema's family and friends. She would also like to thank the FNRS (Fonds de la Recherche Scientifique) for funding a field trip to India in 2009. Special thanks go also to Chris Way from Reality Tours in Mumbai, who was very open and helpful with the research in Dharavi.

We also would like to thank the numerous anonymous people we met during our field trips – tourists or locals who inspired our reflections on tourism and India. We would particularly like to thank Ingo and Ineke Pederson, our 'flashpacker' friends with whom we spent a couple of days in Kerala in January 2009.

The decision to write this book was born in spring 2008 in Shimla at the ATLAS Backpacker conference, hosted by Professor Bansal from Himachal Pradesh University, and we thank Professor Bansal for his kind hospitality. The rather rapid realisation of this book is thanks to Emma Travis and Faye Leerink from Taylor and Francis, who shared our enthusiasm for the project.

Our thanks also go to Marie Mathy, a postgraduate student at the Université Libre de Bruxelles, who at the time of writing stayed in New Delhi for an internship. She was frequently our 'local correspondent' and provided us with new photos and fresh information. We would also like to thank Quentin Rombaux formally for drafting the India map. Of course, any errors or omissions in this book remain ours.

We formally acknowledge the following of the use of their images: Figure 1.1 Reality Tours and Travel; Figure 2.1 Ministry of Tourism, India; Figure 2.2 Kerala Tourism; Figure 2.3 Assam Tourism; Figure 3.1 Reality Tours and Travel; Figure 3.2 Kerala Tourism; Figure 4.3 Marie Mathy; Figure 6.1 Darya Maoz; Figure 8.1 Belleville AG. All other images were taken by the authors.

# 1 Tourism and India

## An ambivalent relationship

### Introduction

India currently stands on the threshold of becoming a major world power. Like Brazil, Russia and China, India has been recognised as playing a crucial role in the future of the world economy. Moreover, globally, tourism has become of central importance to social, cultural and economic lives in the twenty-first century. However, unlike these other countries, India has not been able to harness tourism development to the same extent. Indeed, as a country, India has always had a rather uneasy and ambivalent relationship with tourism. This book thus details the significance of the practices of tourism for India in the twenty-first century. The overarching aim of the book is to help you reach a point of critical understanding about tourism and India rather than for us to simplistically describe the many, various sites of tourism in India. We spent a lot of time pondering the title for this book, and we want to emphasise that it is about tourism and India and not just about tourism in India. This introduction is thus intended not only to welcome you to our book but also to outline the position from which we have written it – the position of the contemporary critical tourism studies literature – we hope in an accessible, readable and enjoyable way. More crucially, however, we wish to present you with a reading experience that will challenge some of your own preconceptions about tourism and India. Although we have divided the book into discrete chapters (to aid reading) we are also cognisant of the ways in which tourism as a cultural activity blurs with or fades into other aspects of contemporary social, cultural, economic and environmental experiences. Moreover, we are also acutely aware of the underlying power relations in tourism production and consumption, as well as how these structures are sometimes transgressed and subverted in the Indian context. We believe that the study of tourism is a vibrant, innovative and interesting academic subject, though you would hardly know so from reading some of the introductory textbooks on tourism and India with their rather bland definitions and descriptions of tourism. Although *Branding India* (2009), the recent account of India's successful 'Incredible India' campaign by Amitabh Kant, the former secretary of India's Ministry of Tourism, is a more positive contribution to these debates, it is still a rather uncritical and polemical account aimed at furthering the tourism business in India.

## Our philosophical approach

We wish to start (and indeed finish) from the perspective that the study of tourism is always difficult and contested. In this context, then, we are acutely aware that the world we live in is fast changing and full of transformations – and India as a country is arguably in the fast lane of these contemporary changes. Thus, this book should be thought of not as the definitive answer to students' questions about tourism and India, but rather as a starting point for an ongoing shared project. Our account of tourism and India draws upon many aspects of post-colonial and post-structuralist philosophy, not because it may be fashionable but because we do find it helps us to understand contemporary tourism and India as a set of complex, negotiated, contingent, blurred and incomplete practices and ideas. We also draw upon the politicised aspects of tourism and tourism development in order to explain the conflicts that frequently arise in India over tourism. Indeed, as Dann (1999: 27) has argued, 'unless issues are problematised – unless we acknowledge that our understanding is incomplete – we will never adequately address issues of tourism development'. We argue that by taking a more sophisticated theoretical approach to the study of tourism and India we may actually hear better the voices of people involved in the practices and processes of tourism development and management.

Moreover, because tourism is integral to processes of globalisation both as an outcome and as a contributing factor, any analysis of tourism needs to take account of theoretical advances in the study of the processes of globalisation. We thus need to understand India in a global context of competing destinations, each of which is trying to position itself with unique selling points. Indeed, it may also be better to think of multiple 'Indias' in this context with a multitude of competing destinations (Goa, Rajasthan, Kerala, Assam, Kashmir) under the 'India' umbrella and with multiple unique selling points. On the other hand, however, processes of globalisation have also led to a degree of homogenisation taking place whereby places become much more similar as a result of the progress of multinational companies selling international brands (fast food outlets are now widespread in India) and international popular culture for international tourists. Nevertheless, we would argue that India retains a remarkable degree of differentiation despite the homogenising processes of globalisation. Many international tourists in India revel both in the exotic and in the everyday and are in search of a series of 'experiences' however imagined.

In this book we are also acutely interested in the behaviour of tourists who visit India themselves. However, our understanding of 'behaviour' does not draw upon psychological models that seek to reduce human behaviour to a simple set of attributes; rather we take a more anthropological approach to understanding behaviour as linked to cultural beliefs, habits and meanings. In so doing, we are also aware that the traditional division between tourism, leisure and everyday life is also blurring with the growth of serious leisure (Stebbins, 2007) and so called 'voluntourism' (Wearing, 2001).

The globalisation of tourism also involves broader political questions and, importantly, the ownership of power (Hall, 1994). Perhaps, as a result, research into tourism has begun to focus more explicitly upon the concept of power itself. In particular, this has meant a shift from the more basic political and economic concepts of power towards an examination of social and cultural relations of power in tourism (Mowforth and Munt, 1998), with particular reference to Foucauldian notions of power (Cheong and Miller, 2000; Hollinshead, 1999). Cheong and Miller (2000: 378), for example, argue that, 'power relationships are located in the seemingly non-political business and banter of tourists and guides, in the operation of codes of ethics, in the design and use of guidebooks, and so on'. And clearly we can see this in evidence in India with the *Lonely Planet* guide exerting a disproportionate effect on many international tourists' behaviour (see also Chapter 6). In terms of tourism development strategies it is recognised that, in addition to participating in the formulation and implementation of tourism ethics, various gatekeepers and brokers discuss and negotiate how far development should proceed, what type of development is optimal, and who should enter as tourists. As we shall see in Chapter 2, this is very important in the context of India as regimes of governance influence the direction of tourism development.

Throughout this book, then, we are also interested in the interplay between metaphor and materiality in tourism and attempt to show that the ways in which people think about the world have implications for the ways in which they then experience tourism in India. However, we do not think that the very stuff of such experiences can be reduced to a simple reading of the materiality of the environment or landscapes of tourism; rather such experiences are fundamentally mediated by a whole host of contemporary media lenses. Moreover, because of the globalisation of mediascapes those in economic need in countries such as India are acutely aware of the desires of others around the world (Shurmer-Smith and Hannam, 1994). Thus, in what follows in this book we concentrate rather a lot upon these mediatised representations and experiences, drawing upon studies of film, literature and advertising, not just because they give pertinent visual illustrations but also because such examples allow us to appreciate the different ways in which people conceive of tourism practices as constitutive of their own identities. Thus, such mediatisations are not simply representations but are also linked with the material conditions of tourism, which certainly need to be problematised. For example, John Hutnyk's (1996) remarkable book *The Rumour of Calcutta* has examined how a combination of tourism representations – literary, photographic, cinematic and cartographic – enframe the tourism experience of Calcutta. Moreover, as we shall see in subsequent chapters, many of these representations of, and in, India rely on 'exotic' social constructions that are frequently manifestations of older colonial, imperial and orientalist desires.

## A critical, contemporary profile of India

As the discussion of globalisation and tourism above has shown, India is clearly positioned in the twenty-first century to become a major economic power and has variously been described as an 'emerging giant' (Panagariya, 2008) or an 'awakening elephant' (Kant, 2009). As Panagariya (2008: xv) notes, '[a] sure fire way to capture the attention of Indian audiences is to tell them that India is destined for stardom in the twenty-first century'. Hence, in this section we wish to outline the key general features of contemporary India in terms of its geography, politics, economics, sociology, culture and environment.

India is highly varied in terms of its physical geography, from the high mountains of the Himalaya to the tropical southern coastal regions, from the vast central plains to the densely forested north-east. India has a distinct monsoon climate with (usually) hot, wet summers and dry, cooler winters interspersed by two very hot and dry months (May and June). The monsoon rains help to feed India's vast rivers and thus support India's agricultural production. The success or failure of the rains can make a huge difference to India's national income in any given year as well as having a profound effect on the seasonality of India's international tourism flows, in particular.

India is also a vast, rapidly developing country with a population of 1.1 billion citizens, who speak eighteen official languages, making it the largest functioning democracy in the world. But it is also a country of vast differences across the twenty-eight states and seven union territories that constitute India's federal system of governance. In terms of economics, India has a gross domestic product (GDP) growth rate in excess of 8 per cent, making it one of the fastest-growing economies in the world. Moreover, India is now much more integrated into the world economy than it was back in the early 1990s and has seen both its exports and its foreign investment multiply in value. Technologically, India has also been transformed in the last twenty years. For example, back in 1991 India had 5 million phone lines; today nearly 600 million Indian people have mobile phones as India's middle class grows, consumes and isolates itself in its own 'housing colonies'. Indeed, as we shall see, India's 'new middle class' (Fernandes, 2007) has been crucial in terms of the development of both domestic tourism and outbound tourism (see Chapters 7 and 8 respectively).

However, against this picture of massive growth and prosperity we also need to note that India still has a great deal of poverty and inequalities (Figure 1.1). Despite an absolute reduction in poverty in recent years, the urban–rural inequalities have worsened. As Panagariya (2008: xxvi) argues: '[t]he ultimate development problem India faces is that of transforming its primarily rural, agrarian economy into a modern one'. The vast majority of the Indian population still lives in rural areas and relies on farming for its livelihood. Moreover, outside of agriculture, 'approximately 90 percent of the workforce remains employed in the informal, unorganized sector' (Panagariya, 2008: xxvi). In addition, these inequalities have been exacerbated by the failure, in part, of the Indian government to deliver effective access to adequate basic social services such as water, education

*Figure 1.1* Street scene in Mumbai.

and health, despite considerable investment (Dreze and Sen, 1995). Varma (2004) meanwhile has accused India's new middle class of a growing amnesia towards this deprivation.

Against this backdrop of contemporary prosperity and poverty, we also need to note the uniquely fractured social structure in India and the ways in which this has been politicised in recent years, often violently. Although ostensibly a 'secular' country that does not advocate any one religion, India's population is over 80 per cent Hindu, with Muslim (14 per cent), Christian (2 per cent), Sikh (2 per cent) and other small minorities, according to the 2001 census of India. Moreover, in recent years India has witnessed the rise of Hindu nationalism, which has included 'state encouraged violence against religious minorities' (Nanda, 2004: 1). Nanda (2004: 2) further argues that, as India modernises technologically, this has only served to 'further an equally aggressive cultural re-traditionalization, visible in the growing influence of religious nationalist ideas on the institutions of civil society and the state'. Nevertheless, as Pinney (2001: 1) notes, despite these internal divisions, there are also many places of shared identity, most particularly in the melodies of Hindi music and in the visual culture of Bollywood films, that transcend the religious and caste divides – something we examine in Chapter 3.

## A statistical overview of tourism and India

One of our central arguments is that, until very recently, the relationship between tourism and India has been characterised by ambivalence and even outright ignorance. However, the situation at the time of writing seems to have begun to change as India's government is much more outward looking and engaged with the global tourism economy. In this section we seek to provide a basic statistical overview of the current state of India's tourism flows to provide an introductory context for the discussions provided in subsequent chapters.

Thus, in terms of figures, India's tourism authority, somewhat ambitiously perhaps, aims to achieve 10 million international tourists in 2010, helped by the Commonwealth Games. In its current *Annual Report*, it also notes that:

> India's performance in tourism sector has been quite impressive. During the period 2002 to 2009, India witnessed an increase in the Foreign Tourist Arrivals (FTAs) from 2.38 million to 5.11 million. Due to global slowdown, terrorist activities, H1N1 influenza pandemic, etc., growth rate in FTAs during 2009 fell by 3.3 per cent. The year witnessed a contraction in global tourism by 4.3 per cent; the declaration in India was, therefore, less than that of the scale of global slowdown.
>
> (Ministry of Tourism, 2010: 7)

Thus, because of the current economic crisis, international tourism arrivals have been lower than envisaged in 2008 and 2009. Indeed, after the terrorist attacks on 25 November 2008, foreign tourist arrivals dropped by several percent until June 2009, when they were balanced again with the previous year (see Table 1.1 for an overview of foreign tourist arrivals 2000–9). The major source countries for foreign tourist arrivals into India are the United States, Canada, the United Kingdom, Australia, France, Germany, Japan, South Korea, Malaysia and Sri Lanka, with tourist inflow from Australia in particular doubling in recent years (ITOPC, 2010).

In terms of overall domestic tourism flows estimates are based upon data collected by state/union territory (UT) governments and are estimated as being 563 million in 2008, a growth of 6.9 per cent over 2007, demonstrating the increased mobility of the Indian population (Ministry of Tourism, 2010) (see Table 1.2).

In terms of actual destinations visited in India, meanwhile, the statistical data for both international and domestic tourists make interesting reading (Table 1.3). The attempt to rank destinations according to the number of visitors is attractive, but must be handled carefully. City states such as New Delhi are compared with geographically large states such as Uttar Pradesh and it is not clear from the statistics how the percentages have been calculated. However, some conclusions may be drawn. It is not surprising that Delhi and Maharashtra are the first destinations for international visitors because most visitors arrive at either Mumbai or New Delhi airport. As 'international visitors' includes everybody and does not distinguish between business and leisure travellers it may be deduced that a large

Table 1.1  Foreign tourist arrivals 2000–9

| Year | Foreign tourist arrivals (millions) | Percentage change over previous year |
|------|------|------|
| 2000 | 2.65 | 6.7 |
| 2001 | 2.54 | −4.2 |
| 2002 | 2.38 | −6.0 |
| 2003 | 2.73 | 14.3 |
| 2004 | 3.46 | 26.8 |
| 2005 | 3.92 | 13.3 |
| 2006 | 4.45 | 13.5 |
| 2007 | 5.08 | 14.3 |
| 2008 | 5.28 | 4.0 |
| 2009 | 5.11* | −3.3 |

Source: Ministry of Tourism (2010).
*Provisional estimate.

Table 1.2  Domestic tourist visits to all states/union territories in India

| Year | Domestic tourist visits (millions) | Percentage change over previous year |
|------|------|------|
| 2000 | 220.11 | 15.4 |
| 2001 | 236.47 | 7.4 |
| 2002 | 269.60 | 14.0 |
| 2003 | 309.04 | 14.6 |
| 2004 | 366.27 | 18.5 |
| 2005 | 391.95 | 7.0 |
| 2006 | 462.31 | 18.0 |
| 2007 | 526.56 | 13.9 |
| 2008* | 562.92 | 6.9 |

Source: Ministry of Tourism (2009a).
*Provisional figures.

number of the visitors to the first three destinations are linked to business because these destinations represent the three major commercial cities in India, namely New Delhi, Mumbai (Maharashtra) and Chennai (Tamil Nadu). Similarly, West Bengal ranks highly in sixth place because it is also a major arrival hub by way of Kolkata.

What may be more surprising is that Rajasthan figures only fifth in the ranking for international visitors, yet it is considered (not least by India's government) to be one of the key destinations for international tourists, and benefits from relatively new tourism infrastructures, although it does not attract as many business

Table 1.3 Destination ranking of international and domestic visitors

| International visitors | | | Domestic visitors | | |
|---|---|---|---|---|---|
| Rank | State/union territory | % | Rank | State/union territory | % |
| 1 | Delhi | 16.6 | 1 | Andra Pradesh | 23.6 |
| 2 | Maharashtra* | 14.6 | 2 | Uttar Pradesh | 22.2 |
| 3 | Tamil Nadu | 14.4 | 3 | Tamil Nadu | 17.5 |
| 4 | Uttar Pradesh | 11.4 | 4 | Rajasthan | 5.0 |
| 5 | Rajasthan | 10.5 | 5 | Madhya Pradesh | 3.9 |
| 6 | West Bengal | 8.0 | 6 | Maharashtra* | 3.7 |
| 7 | Andra Pradesh | 5.6 | 7 | Uttarakhand | 3.6 |
| 8 | Kerala | 4.2 | 8 | West Bengal | 3.4 |
| 9 | Himachal Pradesh | 2.7 | 9 | Gujarat | 2.8 |
| 10 | Goa | 2.5 | 10 | Karnataka | 2.3 |
| | Total of top 10 states | 90.5 | | Total of top 10 states | 88.0 |
| | Others | 9.5 | | Others | 12.0 |
| | Total (total number of people) | 100.0 (14,112,590) | | Total (total number of people) | 100.0 (562,915,569) |

Source: Ministry of Tourism (2009a).
*Figures for Maharashtra have been estimated.

travellers as the major Indian cities. The same statement can be made for Kerala and Goa, for they are also major destinations addressing the international market. Nevertheless, it is significant that Rajasthan, Goa and Kerala all receive ten times more international tourists than domestic tourists (ITOPC, 2010; see also discussion below). The fourth rank of Uttar Pradesh can be explained, in part, by the Taj Mahal in Agra, clearly one of the most important tourist destinations in India (see Chapter 4).

The ranking of destinations when it comes to domestic tourism is clearly a totally different one. Andhra Pradesh is perhaps the first-ranked destination because of its geographic centrality, for many domestic tourists will pass through the state to get to other destinations and stay there en route. Uttar Pradesh, being the largest state in India populationwise, attracts a lot of VFR (visiting friends and relatives) traffic. The relatively new and small state of Uttarakhand, ranked seventh, is significant for domestic tourists as it is the site of many Hindu pilgrimage destinations as well as being a major attraction because of its location for many Bollywood films (see Chapters 7 and 3 respectively).

In terms of Indian tourists venturing abroad, the growth has also been significant, despite the relatively small overall numbers in comparison with the total Indian population (see Table 1.4 and also Chapter 8 for a fuller discussion).

## Structure and content of the book

Both of the authors of this book have extensive field experience of India and we hope to demonstrate this in the chapters that follow through our observations and arguments. As European authors we are also acutely aware of the post-colonial theoretical position from which we write. Readers of this book will also recognise that we also come from a broadly qualitative methodological background and

Table 1.4  Number of outbound Indian tourists 2000–8

| Year | Number of outbound Indian tourists (millions) | Percentage change over the previous year |
|------|-----------------------------------------------|------------------------------------------|
| 2000 | 4.42 | 7.3 |
| 2001 | 4.56 | 3.4 |
| 2002 | 4.94 | 8.2 |
| 2003 | 5.35 | 8.3 |
| 2004 | 6.21 | 16.1 |
| 2005 | 7.18 | 15.6 |
| 2006 | 8.34 | 16.1 |
| 2007 | 9.78 | 17.3 |
| 2008* | 10.65 | 8.8 |

Source: Ministry of Tourism (2009a).
*Provisional figures.

hence we do not provide extensive statistical analyses (except for the above), which we feel are better provided by India's Ministry of Tourism itself. Nevertheless, one of the key aims of the book is to synthesise in one volume a wide range of literature pertaining to tourism and India. Hence, we rely heavily on the research undertaken to date by a wide range of authors. However, we also need to emphasise that on many topics pertaining to tourism and India there is a relative paucity of critical literature, either as a destination, or as a source of tourists, perhaps due to it being a difficult, ambivalent and under-recognised relationship until recent years. Indeed, although India's tourism development differs in many ways from other emerging countries, it is often assessed together with other Asian developing countries and in particular compared with China (see Hall and Page, 2000). Following this introduction there are seven substantive chapters and a conclusion, with each chapter providing a number of boxed sections and images that we hope illustrate the contemporary changes in the relationship between tourism and India.

Chapter 2, entitled 'Governing and promoting tourism in India', critically evaluates the historical and contemporary governance structures that have shaped the current forms of tourism development in India. It thus examines the organisation of the Indian state and its federal governance as it pertains to tourism development. It points out the context of national tourism policies, but also highlights the differences between 'honey pot' states such as Kerala and less promoted states such as Assam. It explores the impact of the recent 'Incredible India' campaign and highlights the changes in recent years in terms of tourism supply, such as the creation of new cultural assets, the revalorisation of heritage assets and adaptation of the tourism industry to international tourism demands and standards.

Chapter 3, 'Cultural tourism in India', then examines the various developments in cultural tourism (defined in its widest sense) that have happened recently in India. Indeed, the Indian government has recently begun to invest in cultural tourism attractions and events to draw in more international visitors. The chapter thus draws upon the contemporary theoretical literature on cultural tourism and events to develop an examination of aspects of both 'conventional' cultural tourism, including the 'arts' such as Bollywood, and the more popular aspects of culture such as contemporary slum tourism. Examples in this chapter are drawn predominantly from the major cities such as New Delhi and Mumbai.

Chapter 4, 'Heritage tourism in India', critically examines the different contemporary conflicts of heritage interpretation and use in India. It will draw theoretically on recent debates on such issues as authenticity, commodification and community involvement to facilitate a more nuanced discussion of some of India's World Heritage Sites (WHS) and its colonial heritage. Key examples of the contestation of heritage tourism in India are drawn from the Taj Mahal, Agra, the temple structures of Mahabilipuram and the Residency at Lucknow. Chapter 5, 'Nature-based tourism in India', meanwhile, critically examines the various contemporary conflicts involved in the use and management of nature-based tourism in India. It draws theoretically upon the concept of political ecology to inform a discussion of these conflicts. Examples are drawn from some of the major national parks in India to illustrate these issues and conflicts.

Moving away from tourism supply to tourism demand, Chapter 6 examines international tourism flows into India. It begins by conceptualising theoretically the discourse of orientalism that has informed many Western representations of India by Western travellers. It then discusses, in particular, how as a predominantly backpacker and religious tourism destination, India has now begun to attract a much broader range of tourists as it has become more attractive as a global destination. It also examines the development of new markets such as medical tourism that have been at the forefront of contemporary tourism developments in India.

As a counterpoint, Chapter 7 then examines the contemporary rise in domestic tourism within India. It draws upon current debates on changing Indian social structures to critically analyse the key trends in domestic tourism in India. Because of the recent economic growth, India's middle class represents a growing consumer group integrating a more westernised lifestyle and benefiting from newly renovated infrastructures and accommodation. Examples are drawn from the resorts of the Himalayan region such as Shimla. Chapter 8, meanwhile, examines the growth of Indian outbound tourism. In relation to this it also evaluates the role and scope of the Indian diaspora in terms of tourism and it draws upon theoretical concepts from the transnational and mobilities literatures to critically analyse this.

## Conclusions

In conclusion to this chapter, we wish to say that we hope that you enjoy the book! But also that if you have any comments or criticisms then please contact us so that we can hopefully make the next edition a better one. Although this text is aimed at an international student readership we particularly welcome critique from Indian academics in the spirit of mutual dialogue. The next chapter considers the governance and marketing of tourism in India.

# 2  Governing and promoting tourism in India

## Introduction

India's recent focus on tourism development is notably due to a new tourism policy offensive being pursued by India's Ministry of Tourism. Although the private sector provides many of the key services such as food and accommodation for tourists in India, it has been the Indian state that has been dominant in ignoring, restricting and, more recently, promoting tourism development in the country. To begin, this chapter conceptualises the notion of state power in relation to tourism more generally. The chapter then highlights the tourism development processes that India has been through in the last twenty years. It will thus examine the organisation of the Indian state and its federal governance as it pertains to tourism development (Hannam, 2004a). It points out the context of national tourism policies and it explores the impact of the recent campaign 'Incredible India' and highlights the changes in recent years in terms of tourism supply, such as the creation of new cultural assets, the revalorisation of heritage assets and the adaptation of the tourism industry to international tourism demands and standards. Finally, the chapter also highlights the regional differences in terms of tourism governance and promotion between 'honey pot' states such as Kerala and less promoted states such as Assam (Hannam, 2005a).

'Tourism has become an integral part of the machinery of many modern governments', write Hall and Jenkins (1995: 1), and tourism has moved to the centre of the regimes of planning within national, local and supranational governments as policy makers have recognised the potential for both income generation and, on the less positive side, environmental damage (Hannam and Knox, 2010). Furthermore, a growing feature of the tourism industry is the extent to which businesses and governments work together to either manage the impacts of tourism or promote or develop tourism in particular destinations. Governments may promote tourism nationally and enact legislation on tourism issues but more generally they regulate the wider economic and cultural environments that tourism operates in (Kerr, 2003). In this context, Hall (1994: 19) argues that:

The functions of the state will affect tourism policy and development to different degrees. However, the degree to which individual functions are related to particular tourism policies and decisions will depend on the specific objectives of institutions, interest groups and significant individuals relative to the policy process.

Many countries are relatively ambivalent about their role in regulating and promoting tourism, preferring to allow the market to have a greater say or to devolve decision making to specialist agencies and local layers of governance. Nevertheless, tourism development has become a key part of many supranational, national and regional strategies, particularly as governments recognise the impact that tourism has on the environment. Various layers of governance also have a significant role to play in the promotion of both tourism and the creative industries as strategies for the regeneration of post-industrial cities and regions. However, literature on the role of the state in these strategies is relatively scarce. As Church and Coles (2007: 278) write: 'tourism studies still lack a full appreciation of the State's current role in relation to tourism and hence its power'. Hence, we believe that what is needed is a more theoretical and historical framework for understanding the role of the state in regulating tourism practices (Hannam and Knox, 2010). We seek to develop this below by considering the notion of the 'state' and then the role of the state in governing, promoting and regulating tourism in India.

## Conceptualising governance in India

We argue that to understand tourism in India and the ways in which the state has both limited and promoted tourism we need to theorise the state, and power relations within it, in some depth. Historically, governance in India during the Mughal period relates to the formation of an imperial state that was relatively high in despotic power and relatively low in disciplinary power. What is usually termed the 'colonial' state in India refers to the authoritarian state established by the British, which was high in terms of the exercise of both despotic and disciplinary power. Finally the emergence of a true bureaucratic state – high in disciplinary power and relatively low in despotic power – rests with the reconfiguration of the Indian state after independence and federalisation (Hannam, 1998).

The exact timings of state transformations in India were tempered by the fact that each province was quasi-autonomous, and each had its own traditions, loyalties and philosophies. Indeed, both Mughal and British governance had been imposed in different regions at different times, with the result that the exercise of power could vary throughout India reflecting the contemporary ideological fashions, political problems or manpower constraints that impinged on the local administration at the time (Cook, 1993). At the same time, however, the extension of state activity from the late nineteenth century onwards disrupted local patterns of power and protest, and made the state more obtrusive and disliked by local communities. It provided new issues and arenas for the ambitious to fight over, and started to link up provincial centres and peripheries as never before.

Hence, the transformation from the Mughal, imperial state to the British authoritarian state was not a straightforward handover following the Indian Mutiny or First War of Indian Independence in 1857. As Cohn (1983) has forcefully argued, this transition was the product of a protracted series of negotiations between British officials and Indian rulers. Many rituals associated with Mughal imperial rule, such as the *durbar*, were integrated into the British authoritarian ritual armoury. At the same time the production of the British state in India was the outcome of concerted philosophical speculation. But this is not to say that the state in India was solely an extension of European thought – we should not underestimate the influence of Indian society in shaping British administration. Indeed, Frykenberg (1979) has emphasised the strength of local influences and tradition in the formation of the British Indian state, arguing that officials had to understand these varied traditions in order to survive. However, although there have been attempts to link the structure of the British civil services in India to the Mughal *mansabdars* or the 'feudal barons', such attempts can also be seen as yet another example of the British concern to place their distinct system of rule within the context of the past (Spear, 1970; Cohn, 1983).

The relationships between the state and society in India can be seen as the product of a series of practices based upon the accumulation of knowledge about India and the creation of disciplinary forms of power. Although it is broadly true to say that the British Indian state was ultimately based upon a monopoly over the means of force and violence, after 1857 only a calculated display of such despotic and coercive power was considered necessary to create an awareness of its authoritarian power (N. Bhattacharya, 1986). In the formulation and implementation of policies and laws, the element of coercion was moderated by the desire to secure consent and conciliate oppositional forces. As a result the legitimising of British rule became the abiding concern of the state, operationalised primarily through various discursive means such as the codification of laws (Washbrook, 1981).

The spaces of resistance to the British authoritarian state in India were ably exploited and stretched by Gandhi's strategies of civil disobedience, non-cooperation and *satyagraha* in the 1920s and 1930s. In addition, the invincibility of the British Indian state was challenged by the nationalist press on moral grounds. Initially, Congress accepted the state apparatus in the same form as the British had fashioned it at the end of the nineteenth century and they ran a protracted campaign, not to destroy it, but to secure increased Indian access to its higher levels. The result was to constantly expand the semi-democratic space in which the Congress operated (Chandra, 1991). As a result the Congress state formation that emerged after independence retained many of the features of the British Indian state but was somewhat different in a number of respects. First, the exercise of despotic power was sharply limited by the introduction of democratic principles. Second, discourses of socialism were introduced in order to transcend traditional practices in Indian society. Third, the nature of administration itself was transformed with Nehru maintaining that a more specialised administration was needed. Fourth, the practice that Nehru and others argued was crucial to their vision of economic development was central or national planning. As Ron Inden (1995: 268) has noted:

> Planning was the utopian principle through which Nehru and his government hoped to embody the foundational Reason of democratic socialism and hence bring about economic development. . . . The utopian practices they proceeded to use, however, were based on the illusion that scientific and technical knowledge were certain and complete and that existing knowledges of the people were of no use.

However, the role of the independent Indian state, whilst increasingly bureaucratic in form, has not remained stable. Indeed, after twenty-five years of national planning, the Indian bureaucratic state formation turned towards ever more subtle, diffused methods of governance involving increased popular participation in the state's activities. Indeed, this has led to reconfigurations in relationships between state and society in India, in line with the processes of 'statisation' noted by Clark and Dear (1984: 60):

> First, the State apparatus may expand by absorbing other components of the State apparatus, or, more interestingly, by absorption of hitherto independent, private regulatory functions within its own rubric. Secondly, an apparatus may attempt to penetrate the interstices of the social contract, thereby extending the domain of social control into diverse social arrangements.

Indeed, during the 1960s and 1970s the Indian state centralised a great deal of governance internally at the expense of internationalisation. However, in responding to changes in the world economy, the Indian state has, since 1985, restructured or liberalised the Indian economy, allowing greater administrative autonomy and a wider role for private finance and entrepreneurship (Pedersen, 2000). Nevertheless, the Indian state still retains many of the features from the colonial period in terms of its apparatus, supplemented by national five-year plans, and it is against this context that we need to examine India's tourism governance.

## Governing tourism in India

The basis for modern India's organised tourism development goes back to 1949 when a 'Tourist Traffic Branch' was established in the Ministry of Transport to deal with issues related to tourism (Ahuja, 1999). In terms of an actual state apparatus it was not until 1958 that the government of India created a separate Ministry of Tourism, albeit one that was attached to the Ministry of Aviation. Tourism at this time was mainly concerned with domestic tourism. The underlying key idea for this early domestic tourism development was to help foster an Indian national identity with the government focused particularly on the creation of numerous youth hostels throughout the country (see Chapter 7). Subsequently, a succession of five-year plans was set up for the development of the tourism sector. The first plans concentrated more on accommodation development. Significantly, between 1980 and 1985, the sixth plan saw the drafting of a new policy on tourism, recognising the importance of domestic tourism and assigning the responsibility of its development to state governments (Ahuja, 1999). Later plans have focused on integrated tourism development 'circuits' resulting in tourism 'hot spots' such as Kovalam, Goa, Gulmarg and Kulu-Manali, which became symbolic models of resort tourism in India (Ahuja, 1999) and the foundations for the later international mass tourism (see Chapter 6).

Like many aspects of the contemporary bureaucratic state in India, the Ministry of Tourism is primarily a hierarchical policy-making executive organisation (S. Singh, 2001) headed by the Minister of Tourism, a politician, and the Director-General (Tourism), a senior member of the Indian Administrative Service (IAS), a career civil servant. Indeed, it is these civil servants, whose history stretches back to the older colonial state apparatus, who exercise considerable power over tourism development or underdevelopment, perhaps more so than India's politicians. The Ministry of Tourism, then, is the nodal agency for the development of tourism in India and seeks to supplement the work of the constituent state governments in promoting tourism (see Box 2.1). However, the Ministry of Tourism primarily concentrates its activities on the needs of foreign tourists whereas the regional governments focus upon domestic tourist needs. The material organisation of tourism development and management in India, however, is structured through a number of key agents, the most important of which is the publicly funded India Tourism Development Corporation (ITDC). The main aim of the ITDC is to assist in developing infrastructure and to help promote India as a tourist destination. Khan (1998: 48) explains that 'it acted as catalyst in the development of tourism by opening up unexplored tourist destinations and creating facilities in remote tourist regions'. Indeed, the ITDC plays a very active role in tourism development, particularly as it also owns the hotel chain Ashok hotels (see Box 2.2).

The first comprehensive tourism policy in India was formulated in 1982 and utilised the notion of promoting selective 'travel circuits' to maximise the economic benefits of tourism: '[t]he plan proposed to achieve intensive development of selected circuits, dispel the tendency of concentration in a few urban centres, encourage the diversification of tourist attractions and opening up economically backward areas which hold many tourist attractions' (Ministry of Tourism, 1999: 2). However, these circuits were based upon heritage and/or religious grounds and largely reflected domestic tourism rather than foreign preferences.

As a result of the economic liberalisation reforms of the 1990s, tourism was singled out as a priority sector for economic investment and a new tourism policy was developed. In 2002, the Ministry of Tourism formulated the National Tourism Policy providing a strategy for tourism development that considered tourism as one of the major elements for national economic growth. Key aspects of this policy were to:

---

**Box 2.1 Functions of the Ministry of Tourism in India**

[The Ministry of Tourism] has a field formation of 20 offices within the country and 14 offices abroad and one sub-ordinate office/project, i.e. Indian Institute of Skiing and Mountaineering (IISM)/Gulmarg Winter Sports Project (GWSP). The overseas offices are primarily responsible for tourism promotion and marketing in their respective areas and the field offices in India are responsible for providing information services to tourists and for monitoring the progress of field projects. The activities of IISM/GWSP have now been revived and various ski and other courses are being conducted in the J&K valley.

The Ministry of Tourism has under its charge a public sector undertaking, the India Tourism Development Corporation, and the following autonomous institutions:

i   Indian Institute of Tourism and Travel Management (IITTM) and National Institute of Water Sports (NIWS).
ii  National Council for Hotel Management and Catering Technology (NCHMCT) and the Institutes of Hotel Management.

The Ministry of Tourism functions as the nodal agency for the development of tourism in the country. It plays a crucial role in coordinating and supplementing the efforts of the State/Union Territory Governments, catalyzing private investment, strengthening promotional and marketing efforts and in providing trained manpower resources.

(http://www.tourism.gov.in/)

---

- Position tourism as a major engine of economic growth;
- Harness the direct and multiplier effects of tourism for employment generation, economic development and providing impetus to rural tourism;
- Focus on domestic tourism as a major driver of tourism growth;
- Position India as a global brand to take advantage of the burgeoning global travel trade and the vast untapped potential of India as a destination;
- Acknowledges the critical role of private sector with government working as a pro-active facilitator and catalyst;
- Create and develop integrated tourism circuits based on India's unique civilisation, heritage, and culture in partnership with States, private sector and other agencies and
- Ensure that the tourist to India gets physically invigorated, mentally rejuvenated, culturally enriched, spiritually elevated and 'feel India from within'.

(Ministry of Tourism, 2002)

## Box 2.2 The Indian Tourism Development Corporation (ITDC)

ITDC came into existence in October 1966 and has been the prime mover in the progressive development, promotion and expansion of tourism in the country. Broadly, the main objectives of the corporation are:

- To construct, take over and manage existing hotels and market hotels, Beach Resorts, Travellers' Lodges/ Restaurants;
- To provide transport, entertainment, shopping and conventional services;
- To produce, distribute, tourist publicity material;
- To render consultancy-cum-managerial services in India and abroad;
- To carry on the business as Full-Fledged Money Changers (FFMC); restricted money changers, etc; and
- To provide innovating, dependable and value for money solutions to the needs of tourism development and engineering industry including providing consultancy and project implementation.

The authorised capital of the Corporation is Rs 75 crores and the paid-up capital as on 31.3.2005 was Rs 67.52 crores. In total, 89.9748% of the paid up equity capital of the Corporation is held in the name of the President of India.

The corporation is running hotels and restaurants at various places for tourists, besides providing transport facilities. In addition, the Corporation is engaged in production, distribution and sale of tourist publicity literature and providing entertainment and duty free shopping facilities to the tourists. The Corporation has diversified into new avenues/innovative services like Full-Fledged Money Changer (FFMC) services, engineering related consultancy services etc. The Ashok Institute of Hospitality & Tourism Management of the Corporation imparts training and education in the field of tourism and hospitality.

Presently, ITDC has a network of eight Ashok Group of Hotels, six Joint Venture Hotels, 2 Restaurants (including one Airport Restaurant), 12 Transport Units, one Tourist Service Station, 37 Duty Free Shops at International as well as Domestic Customs Airports, one Tax Free outlet and two Sound & Light shows.

(http://www.tourism.gov.in/aboutus/ITDC.htm)

More recently (1997–2002) this plan has been interpreted as involving primarily the development of large-scale tourism resorts at selected destinations. However, half of all expenditure is earmarked for overseas marketing and publicity. Developing foreign tourism arrivals is seen as the main focus, partly because of the need for foreign currency. There is, however, some concern about safeguarding against the potentially negative environmental and cultural impacts of tourism. It is also beginning to be recognised that domestic tourism has grown rapidly in recent years, in both size and sophistication, because of the emergence of a dynamic urban middle class with disposable income. The Ministry of Tourism has viewed cultural and heritage tourism as its central focus and aims to provide visitor facilities, particularly for foreign tourists, around specific monuments and heritage sites (see Chapters 3 and 4). It also sees a growing market in pilgrimage tourism for both the domestic and diaspora markets (see Chapters 7 and 8). However, more recently it has also given some limited attention to diversification and the development of nature-based tourism (see Chapter 5).

In early 2009, the Ministry of Tourism launched a new tourism policy emphasising the importance of domestic tourism and allocating new funding to the development of this, as it wishes to continue to 'encourage domestic tourists to visit unexploited tourist destinations in various states and thereby, project India as an attractive multi dimensional tourist destination' (Ministry of Tourism, 2009b: 1). Alongside this, however, it also hopes to open up new markets in neighbouring countries, such as Singapore, Korea and China.

Thus, tourism to, out from and within India has undergone some important changes in recent years. The Indian tourism industry has had to adapt on the one hand to a rising number of international visitors, but also to increasing domestic tourism due to the growth of the middle class within the country. It is also recognised that, as its economy continues to grow at a rapid rate, India will become one of the most important countries in terms of future outbound tourism, as its middle classes look to visit destinations abroad. This has led to the (re)development and (re)branding of many of its destinations as the Indian government has begun to recognise the potential importance of tourism to the Indian economy and has begun to invest in tourism infrastructure (Raguraman, 1998; Bandyopadhyay and Morais, 2005). We will now discuss this contemporary rebranding of India's tourism.

## Developing brand India

A key aspect of India's contemporary tourism governance since 2002 has been a change from a primary function of regulating tourism and the supply of facilities for domestic tourists towards a global destination branding strategy. As Kant (2009: 4) notes: '[u]ntil 2002, India had eighteen tourism offices abroad. There was no positioning, common branding or a clear precise message. One foreign office called it "Spiritual India" another termed it "Cultural India" and the third "Unbelievable India"'. The development of a single 'mother' brand for India's tourism was seen as important in the face of Asian competition following the events of 9/11 (Kant, 2009).

In marketing terms a brand is a unique combination of product characteristics and added values that have taken on a particular meaning in the minds of consumers: 'When consumers make brand choices about products – including destinations – they are making lifestyle statements since they are buying into not only an image but also an emotional relationship' (Morgan and Pritchard, 2002: 12). Indeed, tourism destination brands are reaching beyond the tourism industry and are now seen as integral to wider processes of economic development:

> Many of those brands at the leading edge of destination marketing are seeking to position themselves as place brands, whereby whole countries, states and regions are embarking on brand building initiatives that are inclusive of tourism and economic development.
>
> (Morgan *et al.*, 2002: 4)

Similarly, Morgan and Pritchard (2002: 39) argue that:

> while tourism is just one element of any destination's economy it should be integral to place marketing since it supports and leads the development of a place brand. The creation of celebrity and emotional appeal through a destination brand opens the way for other economic development-oriented agencies to communicate to would-be investors and residents.

Destination branding is viewed as perhaps the most powerful marketing weapon available to contemporary destination marketers confronted by increasing competition. It has been argued that destinations need to create a unique identity as the basis of survival in an increasingly competitive global tourism marketplace (Hannam, 2004b). In their overview, Morgan *et al.* (2002) argue that there are currently a number of key issues facing contemporary tourism marketing in order to develop a successful 'brand'. These are the role of politics, the role of market research, the need to build partnerships and the role of brand 'champions' in driving brand development. In the context of tourism development, perhaps the first is the most pertinent currently as both global and domestic political changes can often unsettle or even thwart marketing campaigns (Hannam, 2004b).

The 'Incredible India' marketing campaign, launched in 2002, thus presented a standardised series of exotic images of Indian architecture, people and landscapes that arguably represented the nation of India (Figure 2.1). These images communicated the diversity and exoticism of India to the Western consumers they were aimed at and thus effectively worked to make the association between India and a sense of wonderment as well as encouraging a growth in international tourist arrivals (Hannam and Knox, 2010). With this campaign, India released a completely new destination management system and established a paradigm shift in terms of its tourism marketing (Kant, 2009). Indeed, one of the key successes of the 'Incredible India' campaign has been that it has helped to change the perception in the West of India as a developing country with 'poverty problems' towards a perception of India as an emerging destination with contemporary values (Bandyopadhyay and Morais, 2005; Kant, 2009). Moreover, Sunil (2009, cited in Kant, 2009: 20) argued that the campaign headlines

*Figure 2.1* 'Incredible India' campaign.

such as 'not all Indians are polite, hospitable and vegetarian' are more than just witty advertising copy. They are symptomatic of a much bigger social phenomenon – an optimistic and extroverted new India, eager to make its presence felt in the global community.

Indeed, Bandyopadhyay and Morais (2005) have highlighted the dissonance between the nationally given image of India and the image India portrays to Western countries, in particular the United States. Based upon an analysis of the Indian government's two marketing campaigns 'Eternally Yours' (1997) and 'Incredible India' (2002) Bandyopadhyay and Morais (2005: 1012) have argued that India's tourism authorities have had a tendency to focus on five major themes:

> personal enlightenment and wellness; cultural diversity reflected in the variety and complexity of its geography and the diversity of its society; the cultural richness demonstrated through the country's diverse architecture and vibrant cultural/religious festivals; the natural beauty of exotic wildlife and scenery; and royal treatment provided with modern comforts.

Meanwhile, in his review of the 'Incredible India' campaign, Amitabh Kant

(2009: 3), the former Joint Secretary in India's Ministry of Tourism, argues that the events of 9/11 were a catalyst in terms of rebranding India as it reminded the Indian government of 'tourism's potential for revenue and employment generation'. He continues that '[t]he lack of consumer demand in 2002 had revealed that Indian tourism lacked a meaningful identity in the global market place, which meant that there was an imperative need to position and brand India as an attractive destination' (Kant, 2009: 3) and he emphasises that the aim of the 'Incredible India' campaign was to create a unified image of India in Western markets. Kant (2009: 16) further notes that the campaign involved

> more than just advertising, which, in fact, played only a marginal role. The brand-building process comprised personal relationships with international tour operators and journalists, partnerships, promotions, contests, use of interactive media and an aggressive communication strategy. . . . In reality, the 'Incredible India' campaign encompassed a new corporate culture.

The 'Incredible India' campaign focused on international markets in three phases:

1  Western and short-haul markets, including the United States, the United Kingdom, France, Spain, Italy, German, Singapore and the United Arab Emirates, that are largely aware of India as a potential destination.
2  Culturally linked markets, including China, Japan and South Korea, that are also aware of India as a potential destination.
3  High-spending international markets, including Russia, that are largely unaware, at present, of India as a potential destination.

One initiative was to use the somewhat negative publicity of the UK *Big Brother* television show to good effect by inviting the show's participants to see India for themselves, which led to much online debate and 'free' publicity (Kant, 2009).

Nevertheless, beyond the branding campaign, there were two other factors that led to the expansion of India's tourism in the twenty-first century, namely the de-regulation of Indian airspace and the sustained growth of India's economy on the world stage. Moreover, parallel to the 'Incredible India' campaign, a domestic tourism campaign entitled *Atithi Devo Bhavah* or *Guest of God* was launched using some of India's leading film actors such as Shah Rukh Khan. This campaign was also focused on tourism service providers in order to try to instil a sense of national pride in tourism delivery (see Chapter 7).

In its most recent annual report, meanwhile, India's Ministry of Tourism (2010) has further articulated its plans for the development and branding of tourism in India. It notes that:

> [t]he Ministry, in its efforts to deliver responsive governance has initiated some measures. It is the first Ministry to have a Performance Agreement signed between the Secretary (Tourism) and the senior officers of the Ministry

of the rank of Joint Secretary and above. This agreement lays down timelines for implementation of specific tasks by the officers. This has culminated in the Results Framework Document for the Ministry being hosted in the official website highlighting its objectives, actions and measurable performance indicators.

(Ministry of Tourism, 2010: 8)

This statement is important as it signifies a shift in terms of tourism governance in India, as well as in the Indian state's thinking more generally, towards a Western system of using performance indicators as a method of public governmentality.

In terms of furthering brand development, meanwhile, the current annual report of the Ministry of Tourism in India also notes the importance of online marketing activities as part of its integrated marketing strategy. Moreover, it 'undertook a series of promotional initiatives to minimise the negative impact of the global economic meltdown and the terrorist attack in Mumbai and to promote tourism to India' (Ministry of Tourism, 2010: 64). These have included various 'roadshows' in developing markets such as Russia, Scandinavia, Australia and the Middle East, focusing, in particular, on showcasing adventure tourism, nature-based tourism, health tourism and sports tourism (emphasising New Delhi hosting the Commonwealth Games), as well as India's cuisine, as niche tourism sectors (Ministry of Tourism, 2010).

India is still far behind many other countries in terms of tourism development, yet official Indian government statements draw out figures that attempt to prove the contrary. In most articles, one finds only a 12 per cent growth rate, compared with the world average of 6 per cent. These statements are based on official United Nations World Tourism Organization (UNWTO) annual reports confirming the relevance of such information. It is, however, surprising that a country that entered the world tourism market in an organised manner at the beginning of the 1990s is still in forty-second place (also according to the UNWTO) when it comes to international tourism. Indeed, the Indian Ministry of Tourism recognises that certain key issues still have to be addressed, such as the relatively poor infrastructure – from the absence of toilets at major monuments to a shortage of rooms (M. Nayar, 2009).

## Developing regional tourism governance

India has a federal system of governance comprising some twenty-eight regional states and seven smaller union territories. Each state and union territory has its own tourism department, each of which has its own regional tourism policy that dovetails with the national tourism policy detailed above. Clearly we do not have space here to consider all of the Indian state tourism policies. Instead we focus on two states that have both been significant in the story of India's tourism governance, namely Kerala and Assam. Whereas Kerala, perhaps, highlights an example of India's tourism governance that has had a mostly positive effect on India's tourism development and position in the global economy, the example of Assam highlights the geopolitical sensitivities of India's tourism governance.

## *Kerala*

Marketed as 'God's Own Country' distinct from the rest of India, and one of the top fifty must-see destinations in the world, Kerala is one of the smallest states in India, but it has the highest density of population (Figure 2.2). Over 30 million people live in Kerala (some 3 per cent of the Indian population), 85 per cent of them living in small villages, which are continuously distributed throughout the state. Approximately 61 per cent of the population are Hindus, 21 per cent Christians and 18 per cent Muslims. Kerala has the highest literacy rate at 91 per cent, the lowest infant mortality rate, the highest life expectancy rate and the highest physical quality of life in India. By India's standards, Kerala is more developed in terms of basic services than other states in India. Indeed, the travel writer Bill McKibben (2009) went as far to say that 'statistically Kerala stands out as the Mount Everest of social development; there's truly no place like it' – a quotation that has been frequently used in publicity for tourism to Kerala. Beneath the surface, however, other writers have emphasised the 'Hoax of God's Own Country', arguing that Kerala, India's model state, is actually hell. They point to Kerala having the highest suicide rate, the highest unemployment rate and the highest crime rate in India (Wadhwa, 2004).

Nevertheless, since the 1980s tourism has been of crucial importance to Kerala's development and has been viewed by the Indian government as demonstrating the importance of place branding more widely (Kant, 2009). However, Kant (2009: 61) is rather scathing in his review of Kerala's initial efforts in terms of tourism, writing that:

*Figure 2.2* Kerala tourism.

In 1995, charters started flying in, bringing in around 10,000 tourists – all of them heading for the beaches of Kovalam. Kerala looked ready to take off – albeit in the wrong direction. The charters accentuated mass tourism. The cluttered, unplanned development in Kovalam, triggered by the backpackers and the 'hippies' of the 1970s, became worse in the wake of mass tourism, which contributed little or nothing to the local economy.

These comments need to be somewhat tempered as research has shown that such tourism has had a significant positive impact on the Keralan economy and that backpackers, in contrast to Kant's observations, spend more in the host country (Hampton, 1998). Hence, in 2005 the Chief Minister of Kerala, Mr Chandy, emphasised that, among other things, 'Tourism drives the State's economy', 'Kerala's economy is largely dependent upon tourism' and even 'Tourism to be the state's new model of development'. Tourism in Kerala has won worldwide publicity and national and regional awards including:

One of the 100 great trips for the 21st Century – 'Travel and Leisure Magazine'

One of the top ten paradises – 'National Geographic Magazine'

One of the top ten holidays for romance – 'Cosmopolitan magazine'

The 'mecca' of the oldest, holistic health system – 'Geo-Saison Magazine'

(Kant, 2009)

According to statistical data from the Department of Tourism, Kerala (2010), there were over 50 million foreign tourist arrivals to Kerala during the year 2008, an increase of 16 per cent over the previous year. Domestic tourist arrivals to Kerala during the year 2008 were nearly 76 million, showing an increase of 14 per cent over the previous year.

However, in its own SWOT analysis the Department of Tourism, Kerala (2002) has argued that Kerala's strengths are that it is relatively peaceful and that it has a well-known brand image, a wide variety of tourism experiences and landscapes, good education and health-care systems, a relatively good transport and communication infrastructure (compared with the rest of India) and relatively few political problems (again compared with the rest of India). Its weaknesses are that it suffers (like most of India) from poor waste management systems, weak quality control mechanisms, militant trade unions (Kerala has had a communist state government for many years) and a high percentage of low-yield foreign tourists – backpackers. The opportunities it has identified are a potential growth in heritage tourism and the development of new markets such as Russia, while as threats it sees environmental pollution, cultural degradation, an over-reliance on tourism in the face of natural disasters and continued competition from other states and countries. Kerala has also been at the forefront of developing traditional, holistic 'health' tourism as part of its 'brand equity' (see Chapter 6). Kerala tourism's

'Tourism Vision 2025' meanwhile has emphasised the need for sustainable tourism development that targets 'alert independent travellers' who are affluent but also interested in responsible tourism as it seeks a new paradigm shift in terms of its tourism development (Kant, 2009). Whether this vision is actually realisable is, however, debatable as Sreekumar and Parayil (2002: 529–530) have argued that 'Kerala's hard won achievements in social development may be unravelling because of serious economic and financial crises that have afflicted the state in recent times'.

## Assam

Geopolitically, Assam's location constitutes a 'frontier' region of strategic importance to India as it has international borders with Bangladesh, Bhutan, China (Tibet) and Myanmar (Burma). Originally encompassing the entire north-eastern region, the state of Assam is today the largest and most populated state (c. 26 million), located in the north-eastern region of India alongside six other states, Arunchal Pradesh, Manipur, Meghalaya, Mizoram, Nagaland and Tripura, and connected only by a narrow 20-km strip of land to the rest of India (the Siliguri Corridor). Baruah (2001: xii) has noted that '[t]he tenuousness of this physical connection underscores the region's cultural and political distance from the Indian heartland'. The region is deemed to be one of the most ethnically and linguistically diverse in India, as well as one of the most politically sensitive as it is also seen as strategically important to the Indian government in terms of maintaining the internal national integrity of India (Figure 2.3).

Assam as a distinct colonial province was formed in 1874 on the basis of largely accidental administrative convenience rather than historical or cultural reasoning. In the early part of the nineteenth century Assam had been viewed largely as an appendage of the province of Bengal. During British administrative reorganisations the name Assam was retained only because of lobbying from the British tea industry, who successfully argued that the word Assam was known in the international tea markets and thus should be retained. Furthermore, the economic and environmental transformation of Assam during the colonial period also led to a significant demographic shift. Colonial officials actively encouraged immigration into Assam because they perceived the Assamese peasantry as being lazy and as showing little interest in the waged labour on offer in the tea plantations (Chatterjee, 2001). Throughout the entire colonial period, the British treated Assam as a land frontier for population migration from the colonial province of Bengal (present-day West Bengal, Bihar, Orissa and Bangladesh). Justifying moves to combine the former areas of Assam and Bengal into a single province, an official said that, 'since Bengal is very densely populated . . . it needs room for expansion and it can expand only eastward' (cited in Baruah, 2001: 39.) In summary, Baruah (2001: 45–46) notes that '[w]hat Assam saw in the late nineteenth century was nothing short of an economic revolution accompanied by massive ecological destruction'.

Following India's independence in 1947, Assam was initially divided into five

*Figure 2.3* Assam tourism.

constituent states. Subsequently, the region was further divided: Nagaland was formed in 1963, Meghalaya in 1970, Mizoram in 1972 and Arunchal Pradesh in 1987. This was more of a top-down process than a response to sustained political mobilisation as elsewhere in India. The prime mover in the break-up of the region was a powerful central government under Indira Gandhi's leadership, which decided that by creating new states it would be able to contain, and even pre-empt, insurgencies in the north-east region. This policy was, however, largely a failure. Indeed, Baruah (2001: 91) argues that '[t]he Assamese have come to see the break-up of Assam as a mark of Assam's lack of control over its own destiny. In recent years, militant Assamese subnationalism has successfully tapped this sense of injury and powerlessness'. This has heightened tensions and led to violence, murder and large numbers of refugees (BBC News, 2003a,b). Moreover, figures on immigrants into Assam have become the source of intense political contestation to the extent that the 1981 census was not conducted in Assam at all. According to the 1991 census, however, out of a total population of over 22 million, nearly 13 million speak Assamese and nearly 5 million speak Bengali as their first language. A further million speak Hindi and another million regard the Bodo tribal language as their mother tongue. In terms of religion, 67 per cent of the present population are Hindu, 28 per cent are Muslim and 3 per cent are Christian (Baruah, 2001).

The actual conflict in Assam in the post-independence period started in 1960–1 when the so-called 'language riots' took place – violent conflicts between ethnic Assamese and Hindu Bengalis that led to many deaths. The insurgency in Assam began in earnest in 1979 and was at its height in the late 1980s, when kidnappings, ransom demands and murders transformed the idyllic life of tea plantation (garden) managers into an insecure one. In March 1983, more than 3,000 people (mostly Muslims of Bengali descent) were killed during election violence (Baruah, 2001). On 15 August 1985 the Indian government (under Rajiv Gandhi) and the Assam movement leaders agreed a compromise – the so-called Assam Accord: 'a broad settlement that included . . . significant promises on key economic and developmental concerns that had animated Assamese subnational politics' (Baruah, 2001: 116). The Accord was not easy to implement, however, not least because the Bodo people felt disenfranchised and continued their violent protests. The Bodo movement claim that Assam is in fact illegally occupied by the so-called Assamese and have called for a separate Indian state called Bodoland since 1987. In total it has been estimated that over 10,000 people have died as a result of the ethnic violence in Assam since the 1980s, most notably because of fighting between the United Liberation Front of Asom (Assam) or ULFA and the Indian military (BBC News, 2004).

Today, Assam remains on high alert; even though the insurgency has been somewhat contained, the political climate in Assam remains unstable with tea plantation managers being routinely murdered (BBC News, 2003c,d,e). The Indian government has vowed to deal firmly with the ULFA and has deployed the army to guard the tea estates, protect executives and ensure continuing foreign investment (BBC News, 2003f,g). The Indian and Burmese armies have also mounted joint counter-offensives against ULFA's bases in Burma (BBC News, 2004). Nevertheless, the ULFA continues to mount attacks that kill people (Bhaumik, 2008) and it is against this backdrop that we must examine the politics of tourism development in Assam.

The number of tourists visiting Assam is, of course, fairly low because of the political instability in the region, with current estimates of foreign arrivals being approximately 140,000 per year (Assam Tourism, 2010). In terms of tourism resources, Assam is famous for its tea gardens and the rare one-horned rhinoceros. Hitherto, the latter has been utilised in Assam for tourism development more than the former – some 62 per cent of domestic and 81 per cent of foreign tourists visit Kaziranga National Park whilst in Assam (P. Bhattacharya, 2001). Since the beginning of the twentieth century, though, Assam was recognised as being of increasing importance to the Indian government in terms of tourism development with some 10 per cent of the Ministry of Tourism's budget continuing to be allocated to the development of tourism in this region (Ministry of Tourism, 2000, 2010).

Nevertheless, despite the government of India attaching great importance to the development of tourism in the north-eastern region, India's national tourism policies (Ministry of Tourism, 2000, 2010) have represented the north-east, and Assam with it, as a largely undeveloped region with many 'potential' tourism resources – particularly in terms of nature-based tourism (see Chapter 5) – but lacking in key tourism 'facilities'. Earlier government policies thus described the north-east region of India thus:

> The rich natural beauty, serenity and exotic flora and fauna of the area are invaluable resources for the development of eco-tourism. The region is endowed with diverse tourist attractions and each State has its own distinct features. The attractions are scattered over the entire region and are largely

located in remote areas within highly fragile environments. These attractions and the people of the region constitute the tourism resources at large. The facilities for stay, food, shopping and entertainment are either non-existent or mostly primitive in nature.

(Ministry of Tourism, 2000: 53)

To further 'develop' the tourism infrastructure in the north-eastern region, the Ministry of Tourism has sought to upgrade state-owned tourist accommodation and refurbish specific tourist attractions. In 2002 it also developed a marketing strategy for the north-eastern region with the slogan 'India's North East: paradise unexplored', in order to lure both domestic and international visitors (Ministry of Tourism and Culture, 2002: 136). Such representations clearly draw a veil over the complex political situation in Assam. Culturally, Assam and the north-east region of India continue to act as India's internal 'Other'. Indeed, local interest groups in Assam blame the lack of development take-up on the difficulties in engaging with corrupt central and regional government bureaucracies (interviews with government officers, Guwahati, 2003, New Delhi, 2003, 2004). Thus, significantly, the overall picture over the past few years is of declining tourist development assistance to the north-eastern region of India and the state of Assam in particular, against a backdrop of increasing government claims that it is doing more to develop the region's tourism infrastructure. The Indian government blames the insurgency and unrest in the state for it not being able to take concrete development initiatives (Voice of Assam, 2010).

## Conclusions

This chapter has foregrounded the significance of the political governance of India's tourism development. It has argued that India's recent focus on tourism development is notably due to a new tourism policy offensive being pursued by India's Ministry of Tourism. Although the private sector provides many of the key services such as food and accommodation for tourists in India, it has been the Indian state that has been dominant in ignoring, restricting and, more recently, promoting tourism development in the country. To begin, this chapter has conceptualised the notion of state power in relation to tourism more generally. It has then examined the historical organisation of the Indian state and its federal governance as it pertains to tourism development. The chapter has discussed India's national tourism policies, exploring the impact of the recent 'Incredible India' campaign. Finally, this chapter has also highlighted the politicised regional differences in terms of tourism governance and promotion between 'honey pot' states such as Kerala and less promoted states such as Assam. In the next chapter we consider aspects of cultural tourism in India.

# 3 Cultural tourism in India

## Introduction

Cultural tourism covers a broad variety of cultural activities from high cultural activities such as the arts to more everyday and even mundane and familiar populist activities through to the advent of so-called creative tourism activities and events. Covering all of these activities may need a whole book by itself; instead we focus in this chapter on just a few pertinent examples of twenty-first-century cultural tourism in India. The Indian government has recently begun to invest in cultural tourism attractions and events such as the Commonwealth Games, due to be held in Delhi in October 2010, to draw in more international visitors in particular (see also Chapters 6 and 8 in particular).

The chapter will thus draw upon the contemporary theoretical literature on cultural tourism and events to develop a coherent examination of aspects of 'conventional' cultural tourism, such as the 'arts' as in Bollywood film tourism, the contradictions of slum tours as a contested form of 'everyday' cultural tourism, and the ways in which dance is embodied and performed as a cultural tourism activity by both hosts and guests in India. Of course, this chapter links into Chapter 4 on heritage tourism and Chapter 5 on nature-based tourism. It also links with Chapters 6, 7 and 8 on international tourism, domestic tourism and tourism mobilities respectively. The focus of this chapter, though, is on the actual production of cultural tourism in India. First of all, however, we seek to discuss recent conceptualisations of cultural tourism in the academic literature before going on to discuss particular aspects of cultural tourism in India.

In her recent text, *Issues in Cultural Tourism Studies*, Melanie Smith (2009: 1) argues that:

> The first stage in any discussion of cultural tourism is therefore the troublesome task of defining culture, which is notoriously problematic as it has both global and local significance, and it can be deeply historic or highly contemporary. It can be represented as physical and material, tangible or intangible; as political and symbolic, or as the practices of everyday life. It is also articulated differently by the numerous stakeholders involved directly or indirectly in the processes of cultural tourism development.

Indeed, both of the authors of this book have argued sometimes over each of their interpretations of what is and what is not cultural tourism! Ivanovic (2009: 43) suggests that everyday 'cultural tourism encompasses both the passive consumption of culture (soaking up the atmosphere of a place or the everyday life) and active consumption of culture (visit to a museum)'. In our 'post-modern' world the neat distinctions between high and low cultural activities have been broken down and cultural tourism is no longer equated with simply the arts or heritage (see Chapter 5 on the latter). Cultural tourism therefore covers 'not just the consumption of the cultural products of the past, but also of contemporary culture or the "way of life" of a people or region' (Richards, 2001: 7), and needs to be understood as an umbrella term for all tourism activities with a cultural focus (McKercher and Du Cros, 2002; M. K. Smith, 2009).

In many instances the tourist consumption of a destination involves not just the visits to primary tourist attractions such as national collections of art, theatres and concert halls, museums and heritage centres, but also the consumption of what we might call secondary tourist facilities (Jansen-Verbeke, 1986). These public spaces, restaurants, cafes, bars, shopping areas and streetscapes are in some cases elevated to primary tourist attractions. This is the case, for example, when the feel or ambience of a city is part of the attraction and original motivation for the tourist. Recent developments in urban tourism evidence the changing demand for a more integrated and lifestyle-orientated approach to a city (Diekmann and Maulet, 2010). Visitors want to experience the atmosphere of a city rather than visit simply the 'classic' tourism heritage assets. A visit to Delhi is therefore as much about shopping, eating and drinking in Connaught Place and walking in parks as it is about a visit to the Red Fort. In part, this is about an attempt to consume the everyday lives of other people and other places as a marker of authenticity. As we shall see, many international travellers wish to 'go native' or experience a city as it is lived by those who reside there, but their participation in that everyday life changes the nature of the spaces and places in which they attempt to take part. Maitland (2007) details how such interactions between hosts and guests lead to the production of new spaces, atmospheres and experiences through the emergence of conviviality. Interactions between tourists and locals are, of course, two-way relationships with each group consuming elements of the lives of the other group. This is what we mean by 'everyday cultural tourism' (Hannam and Knox, 2010).

A much more imbalanced relationship occurs in this 'everyday cultural tourism' when tourists visit the everyday working lives of other people. Factory tours can be voyeuristic insights not only into how consumer goods are produced, but also into the lives of those involved in the labour process. The labour process itself becomes a commodity as it is rendered as something to be observed or photographed. Other occupations, however, do attract aspirational and admiring visitors when they present themselves as public, tourist spectacles. This is the consumption of the everyday reality of other people without the tourist having either the opportunity or the desire to actually live out those experiences (Hannam and Knox, 2010). We discuss this below in terms of the so-called 'slum tours'.

First, we will examine a rather different form of cultural tourism in India, namely the so-called 'Bollywood tourism'.

## Bollywood – film and cultural tourism in India

In India, the production and consumption of films are central to the everyday experience of 'cultural tourism' for both domestic and international travellers. In her book, *Film-Induced Tourism*, Sue Beeton (2005: 10–11) produced a typology of forms and characteristics of film tourism. These include:

- film tourism as primary travel motivator (when the film site is the attraction in its own right);
- film tourism as part of a holiday;
- film tourism pilgrimage (paying 'homage' to a film including re-enacting scenes);
- celebrity film tourism (visiting homes of celebrities or film locations with celebrity status);
- nostalgic film tourism (visiting film locations from a previous era);
- constructed film tourism attractions (constructed after the filming to attract tourists);
- film and movie tours of specific locational sites;
- film tourism to places where the filming is only believed to have taken place (rather than where it actually did take place);
- film tourism to where the film is set but not actually filmed;
- film studio tours (where the actual filming may be watched);
- film studio theme parks (usually adjacent to an actual film studio);
- visits to movie premieres;
- film festivals.

This form of cultural tourism has recently attracted researchers in particular for its importance for place branding (Hudson and Ritchie, 2006). Places where movies are shot become tourist attractions by themselves, but film tourism consists not only of visits to 'on location' film sites, but also of visits to studios off location (Beeton, 2005). Whereas some studios have developed tourism theme parks where they display settings of their famous movies, others, such as Paramount studios, take visitors on a tour through actual shootings and works related to the film industry. However, as we shall see in the case of Bollywood, some of these trends are followed for reasons other than are given by their American counterparts and for other target markets.

'Bollywood', a term linking Hollywood and Bombay, produces around a thousand films each year and, as such, it is arguably the most important film industry in the world. Vasudevan (2003: 86) notes that: '[t]he question of Bollywood is a complex one, addressing issues of globalisation, the state's cultural policies, new linkages between cinema, fashion, advertising and music, and a new constellation of commodity culture'. Moreover, Bollywood also plays a major role in the social construction of India's national identity. Indeed, Varma (2004: 154–155) states that:

> Bollywood has been the single biggest integrating factor of the Pan-Indian person. . . . Whatever their language, Indian films belong unmistakably to one genre, and cumulatively project a world in which all Indians can participate. Their largely escapist fare is inclusive for its deliberate avoidance of high-brow aesthetics. Their fantasies provide a few hours of relief to the ordinary Indian besieged by problems of everyday life. And their happy endings and dances provide a kind of entertainment with which all Indians identify.

More recently the Indian film industry has targeted the Indian diaspora by creating emotional and nostalgic links between non-resident Indians (NRIs) and people of Indian origin (PIOs) and the home country (Bandyopadhyay, 2008; Tirumala, 2009; see also Chapter 8). One reason for this is the development of the content of the films. Up until the 1990s, Bollywood films mainly addressed the Indian home public. Since then the contents of the films have changed considerably: aspects of modern urban life in India and the Indian diaspora have become important themes with the latter portrayed as 'exiled' Indians longing for and rediscovering their roots back home (Bandyopadhyay, 2008; Vasudevan, 2003).

In particular, films that did not have a major success in India, such as *Kal Ho Na Ho* (2003) and *Swades: We, the People* (2004), have become major films within the diaspora (for a synopsis of the latter, see Box 3.1). These films draw on nostalgia while also portraying a modern and developed India, and both NRIs and POIs have expressed their wish not only to visit the country, but also to visit the film sites (Bandyopadhyay, 2008). It should be added that, in contrast to Western countries where film locations and theme parks are mass tourist attractions (Gladstone and Fainstein, 2001), Bollywood settings and studios are still a rather cost-intensive 'niche sector'.

In this context, the sociologist Jean Baudrillard (1994: 9) has noted the ways in which in the contemporary world we can now produce copies of places and

---

**Box 3.1  Synopsis of the film *Swades: We, the People***

Set in modern day India, *Swades* is a film that tackles the issues that development throws up on a grass root level. It is to this India, which is colorful, heterogeneous and complex that Mohan Bhargava (Shah Rukh Khan), a bright young scientist working as a project manager for NASA, returns to on a quest to find his childhood nanny.

The film uses the contrast between the highly developed world of NASA . . . and the world back home in India to highlight the metaphysical and elusive search for home.

(http://www.swades.com/html/film.html)

objects that may seem better or more real than the original – hyper-reality. As an example he discusses the caves at Lascaux in France covered in prehistoric paintings. When the paintings in the cave began to show signs of decay as a result of the numerous visitors, a duplication was rendered close by so that sightseers could appreciate the site without destroying it . . . and without actually seeing it. The duplicated tourist experience became the real tourist experience. We find this same process occurring in Bollywood with replica studios such as the Bollywood Drome being built explicitly for the tourist market (see Box 3.2).

Another important aspect of the Indian film industry is the outplacement of movie settings as well as of important events. Significantly, Indian cinema films

---

**Box 3.2  A Bollywood tourism package tour**

The Bollywood Tourism Package is day long, split into two sessions.

1st session: Bollywood Drome

Immerse yourself in the world of your favourite movies.

A specially created studio called BollywooDrome has been designed for the tour – with sets created to recreate memorable Hindi movie scenes.

It will be an interactive and participative session with performers, directors and technicians from Bollywood who will enact scenes from movies for the visitors, along with a question and answer session.

Action sequences – film technicians demonstrate how stunts and fight scenes are executed and finally how it appears on the screen.

Dance sequences – choreographers recreate the dance magic of movies with a demonstration on how it is done.

Scenes from movies – performers with a director will enact scenes and demonstrate techniques.

Q & A sessions – visitors can ask questions and get answered by a panel of technician.

Interval: Lunch at BollywooDrome in the style of a unit lunch.

2nd session: On the sets

An intimate exposure to the behind-the-scenes activities of a movie or a teleserial. Get an inside look at the sets and what goes into the making of movies. Or get to watch capable technicians work on a movie at a post production studio. Watch a likely hit of tomorrow being shot and get a feel of the movie and the television industry. Night stay in Mumbai.

(http://www.tajmahaltours.com/goldentriangle-bollywood.htm)

have made use of particular landscapes as settings for their storytelling. Dwyer and Patel (2002: 59) note that:

> Overseas locations were first used in [Indian cinema] films in the 1960s, as colour film encouraged the use of landscape as spectacle. . . . In these films travel represented the exotic and Utopias of consumption for a range of lifestyle opportunities and consumerist behaviour, not least owing to the prohibitive cost of foreign travel.

Moreover, Brockmann (2002: 21) has noted that the Swiss Alpine mountains are used primarily 'as a screen on to which emotions can be projected'. As Rachel Dwyer (2001: 25–27) adds:

> In the Hindi movie, love is expressed in particular settings. They are usually pastoral, that is in a city dweller's imagined form of the countryside. . . . Switzerland in Hindi films does share some of the features of Kashmir – a pastoral idyll of mountains and tamed nature that is ideally suited to the traditional landscape of love. Switzerland is the Indian version of pastoral.

Of course, the mountains of Kashmir have a wider political and symbolic meaning for much of the Indian population. Nevertheless, and as we shall see in Chapter 8, Switzerland and countries with similar landscapes have been the first focus for Indian middle-class outward-bound tourism since the 1990s. Furthermore, in 2007, just before the International Indian Film Academy Awards (IIFA) (Bollywood's equivalent of the Oscars) held in Yorkshire, England, Visit Britain launched a map with important Bollywood movie settings throughout the UK, targeted at the Indian diaspora.

Connecting our discussion of Bollywood tourism as a central part of the cultural tourism experience of India – mostly for domestic and non-resident Indian visitors – is also the mediatised experience that many Western visitors have of India prior to their visit. Many Western visitors first experience 'India' through Western film portrayals of India (Mitra, 1999), first as a child watching Disney's *The Jungle Book* and later as an adult watching films such as *City of Joy* and, more recently, *Slumdog Millionaire*. We go on to discuss the impact of these later films below in terms of the touristic experience of so-called 'slum tourism'.

## Slum tourism

Slum tourism is not an invention new to India, but a practice that was originally created by the European upper classes from the late seventeenth century onwards as a recreational pastime. At this time visiting the poor areas of a town or city represented an escape backed by a romantic imaginary. In the nineteenth century slum tours became a much more organised undertaking. In the last decade of the nineteenth century, for instance, Baedeker's *London and Its Environs* (1887) included alongside the conventional heritage attractions 'excursions to world renowned philanthropic institutions in notorious slum districts such as Whitechapel and Shoreditch' (Koven, 2004: xx). Even Charles Dickens undertook slum tours of New York back in the nineteenth century as part of his research for his novel writing.

Today there is a renewed interest in visiting the poorest areas of cities as a form of everyday cultural tourism. But in contrast to nineteenth-century slum tours, contemporary tourists tend to visit those in developing countries. In the 1990s the first slum tours began with organised visits to the *favelas* in Brazil. Indeed, the *favela* Rocinha in Rio led successful campaigns and is now the third most popular tourist attraction in the city (Williams, 2008). Today there are numerous tours and hostels in the *favelas* and since then so-called slum tourism has developed in both Africa and the Indian subcontinent. In South Africa, slum tourism is sometimes assimilated with township tourism; however, one major point distinguishes the two: whereas tourism in townships such as Soweto is very much related to identity and the symbolism of the freedom fight of the black community in South Africa, slums elsewhere generally do not have any other symbolic feature than to be the forgotten part of a city. They are areas with extremely poor living and social conditions. So why would tourists want to visit these places?

The contemporary cultural phenomenon of slum tourism is either highly criticised and condemned as voyeurism or understood as the only possibility to encounter the 'real' side of a particular country (Hutnyk, 1996). Most of the moral and ethical judging has been fairly journalistic, with many Western-authored articles referring to so-called 'poverty tourism' or even 'poverty porn' in a particularly negative way, treating the visitors as voyeurs demeaning poor people (Selinger and Outterson, 2009). However, Selinger and Outterson (2009: xx) also acknowledge that some online visitors voice other concerns about the ways in which slum tours may also obscure wider issues about global inequalities. As Hutnyk (1996: 21) points out: 'Even among those who acknowledge the realities of economic disparities between travellers and toured, a degree of consumption of poverty is inevitable and can contribute to a maintenance of that poverty as a subject of "observation"'.

Nevertheless, they also point out that 'slum tours' also lead many visitors to actually reflect and debate issues of global ethics in ways in which they may not have done beforehand. Indeed, Hutnyk (1996) has noted that some Western travellers self-reflect on their time in India when undertaking volunteer work there, with the ironic label of 'sick tours'. Furthermore, they also note that many discussions of slum tours have had a tendency to reduce and homogenise the reactions of 'hosts' to those that visit the slums. Instead, we need to recognise that some are pleased to see tourists and others are indifferent and still others are openly hostile. This also has pertinent links with contemporary debates over the conflicting values also involved in volunteer tourism, in which asymmetric presence is similarly clearly contested (Wearing, 2001). Clearly, like volunteer tourism, slum tours can be potentially damaging for both hosts and guests if they have a tendency towards a superficial engagement that is wholly commodified. As Selinger and Outterson (2009) observe, active consent on the part of hosts is vital for any slum tourism to have a cultural meaning for both the guests and, indeed, the hosts.

Since the films *City of Joy* and *Slumdog Millionaire* were released, slum tourism has become a buzzword, especially as these Western films' portrayals of poverty in the cities of Calcutta (Kolkata) and Mumbai, respectively, were widely criticised by the Indian media for their sentimentalisation and romanticisation. Both of these 'feel-good' films have been highly popular, particular in the West, but both have drawn critical scrutiny, particularly in India. Indeed, they contrast starkly with the representations of modern India portrayed in contemporary middle-class Bollywood films. Thus, in both research and the media, visits to slums mainly appear to be just another form (or perversion) of tourism, and yet the activity of visiting places that the visitor would prefer not to live in, or could not even consider living in, goes far beyond the categorisation of slum visits as a simple but controversial tourism activity that stresses the boundaries between the rich and the poor, with the latter becoming objects of pity and/or compassion. It questions the commodification of poverty and the turning of poverty into a touristic product (Freire-Meideros, 2009).

In what follows, we discuss slum tours in India by drawing upon examples from Mumbai and Delhi. In recognising the controversial nature of this type of tourism, we believe that, before condemning it, ethical issues and impacts on the hosts should be analysed. In this context, we also wanted to know why people go to visit slums. As the anthropologist Berger (2008: 21) notes:

> [t]he extremes of beauty which many tourists seek require extremes of ugly to be meaningful . . . many tourists find that their experiences in India give them a new respect for all people and an appreciation of the incredible difficulties many of them face as they struggle, heroically in some cases, to survive.

Slum tourism has some connections with recent investigations into 'dark tourism' with the latter focusing on death rather than poverty. However, even the vast dark tourism literature has struggled to uncover the motivations of tourists for visiting these sites (Stone, 2006; Rolfes, 2009). Both slum tourism and dark tourism are ambivalent touristic experiences – the tourist both wants and does not want to visit places such as slums or Nazi concentration camps. Julia Kristeva (1982) has argued that this is because the Western tourist is caught up with his or her own sense of abjection in engaging with these sites. Peter Nyers (2003) has used the phrase 'abject cosmopolitanism' to explain this phenomenon whereby the Western cosmopolitan elite look down upon the poor inhabiting the slums in 'abject poverty'. However, this dualism between the tourist who gazes and the object of poverty is too neat. In fact, our research has found that it is rather the tourist who feels abject and out of place in the slums 'on tour' while the seemingly 'abject' host is in place and not abject at all. People who live in so-called 'abject poverty' seem to get on with their lives; it is the figure of the emancipated Western tourist who is abject in relation to the poverty and disorder that he or she encounters. Following Mary Douglas (1966), the engagement with dirt and poverty is based not on any hygienic anxiety but rather on an arbitrary paradigm that presents itself as an economy of the sacred and profane (Brayton, 2007). We discuss this further below in a couple of examples.

Mumbai with its 12 million people has numerous slums with very varying degrees of living standards, from simple plastic sheds with electrical power and a water supply to almost nothing at all. The largest slum in the centre of Mumbai is called Dharavi, and has the rather dubious honour of being known as the largest slum in India, with around 600,000 households (Municipal Corporation of Greater Mumbai, 2010). It does not feature on official maps, but is located on what is presently very expensive land in the district of Bandra. This is somewhat ironic as the poorest live in the same municipality as the richest, for many Bollywood stars also live in Bandra. However, Dharavi is one of the 'better' slums because it has a water supply for three hours a day and has electricity. It should be stressed that most of Dharavi does not necessarily correspond to how people imagine a slum – unplanned plastic shacks – but instead is a built environment that is not so very different from other urban or rural environments in India. As Kalpana Sharma (2000: xxxv) writes: '[w]hat marks Dharavi from other slums is also its productivity. It is more like an industrial estate than a slum, except people live and work in the same place'.

Since 2006 Reality Tours and Travel has offered slum tours of a part of Dharavi (see Box 3.3). The tours are around two hours in length on foot around a mainly Muslim section of the area with a guide who seeks to explain the daily life, work and industries in the slum. The tours are made up of small groups of around

---

**Box 3.3  Reality Tours and Travel**

We think that Dharavi, the biggest slum in Asia, is one of the most interesting places to see in Mumbai. A few visitors such as Prince Charles and Bill Clinton have been to Dharavi, and it is by no means dangerous to go alone, but the beauty of Dharavi lies not on the main roads but in the small hidden alleys where thousands work and live in a number of small enterprises, where goats roam freely and where children play with carefree abandon.

One of our guides, who all speak very good English and have a wide knowledge of the area, will explain the industry and talk about the people including the issues that they face. You are encouraged to ask questions! We want the tour to be as comfortable for you as possible and so we have a NO TIPS POLICY. The guides are paid a good wage and are rewarded on the basis of the questionnaires which we ask everybody to fill out after the tour.

(http://www.realitytoursandtravel.com/)

six people with a no photography policy. The philosophy of Reality Tours is to improve and/or change the image of slums and expose the sense of community and organisation within the district. A total of 80 per cent of the tour fee is reinvested in a community centre developed by Reality Tours. Although the tours are arguably 'sensitive' they also highlight the playing out of the prioritisation of needs, wants and desires in the contemporary global tourism system as locals are pulled into a global mediatised world – in the case of *Slumdog Millionaire* rather literally with local cast members being whisked off to Hollywood and then returned back to the slums.

The second example is drawn from Delhi, where the non-governmental organisation (NGO) Salaam Baalak Trust organises tours from the Delhi central train station amongst street children. It declares that its principal aim is to offer centres and contact points for street children living in and around the station to promote education in order to help them to become responsible citizens and to be able to make their own living without recourse to begging. The NGO has five centres where children can live and six contact points spread throughout the city where children can get food, relax, wash and study. It also aims, however, to sensitise tourists and of course raise some funds. Since 2003 a City Walk has been created in order to provide the street children with the opportunity to share their experiences and practise their English. Tourists are taken on a two-hour walk in the neighbourhood of the Delhi station and the guide presents the charity's cause by sharing the narratives of the street children with the tourists. As at Dharavi photos are not allowed.

In both cases discussed above, in order to provide an 'authentic' experience for the tourists, most of the guides either come from the slum areas themselves or are 'former' street children. In both cases the tourists are welcomed by the hosts, although it is difficult to judge what preparations go on behind the scene before the visits. Both tours could appear to be intrusive; however, in neither tour are private places accessible. Nevertheless, through the personal contact with the guide, the tourist is helped to be at ease, which ultimately makes the experience a positive one for the tourist as demonstrated by the feedback given by the visitors in questionnaires administered by the two organisations.

Debating slum tours, however, always implies ethical and moral questioning about the practice itself, however comfortable the visitor might feel. The aim is not to give a value judgement, but to analyse and highlight the motivations and experiences of visitors and to provide some empirical evidence to the current media debate. Our own research has demonstrated that the vast majority of visitors are Western tourists through all age groups: from backpackers through to the 'cultural tourist' in his or her late fifties. About one-third of all visitors come through friends and relatives (often ex-pats) they are visiting in Mumbai or Delhi. Others come either by way of the Internet or *Lonely Planet*, one of the few guidebooks that mention the tours. In contrast to the general allegations made by the press and on most blogs, of voyeuristic visits with the aim of looking at the poor, the responses we gathered from visitors to Dharavi emphasised their ambivalences and sensitivities to the whole issue of slum tours. Research, a deeper understanding of India and a search for 'authentic' social encounters were all provided as explanations for their visits to the slums. Yet, clearly, these tourists are also visiting as part of their own journeys to find themselves and there is also a romantic edge to their comments. The few domestic tourists that make their way as visitors to Dharavi also consider this sort of visit as essential to their understanding of the metropolitan experience (Figure 3.1).

Although the experience is largely a positive one, many Western visitors arrive with a slightly uncomfortable feeling for they have difficulties in evaluating their positionality in relation to the people they are visiting. The attention given by the guides during the visit, however, comforts the visitors and provides an impression of ethically correct conduct. For example:

> I was joyful and excited to be able to share a moment with these persons. After the tour the same feelings were still there. The visit of the slum has been a great cultural interchange. I had been able to speak, laugh with everyone . . . even the guide was surprised about the easiness I and the people were interacting.
>
> (Italian, 31)

*Figure 3.1* Dharavi, Mumbai.

After the visit I felt a sense of happiness and that I had increased my knowledge of a different culture. I was amazed at the pride the people had with their surroundings, and felt that if I was in Mumbai longer I would offer my services to the Reality Tour group to help with education.

(British, 26)

Urry (1990/2002) has conceptualised the post-modern tourist who has an inherent detachment from the places he or she visits and who is aware of the performances of hosts and accepts staged authenticity. Yet, in the case of slum tours, comfort zones are challenged and a wish to go beyond commodified attractions is expressed by the simple act of going to the slums. How far the visit is a performed act is difficult to judge, although the number of people met and the size of the district visited makes a staged performance difficult. The practice of slum tourism shows the fine balance between the commodification of culture and the search for 'authentic' experiences as well as highlighting the difficult power relations that underlie much 'cultural tourism'. In our next example of cultural tourism in India we examine this notion of performance in more detail.

## Performing cultural tourism – dancing in India

Some aspects of cultural tourism easily lend themselves to being described as performances, such as the films discussed above. The notion of performance, however, has a much wider and more significant meaning in the social sciences than simply those times when people dress up in costumes and follow scripts, act on a stage, or sing and dance. As we have already noted, tourism as cultural activity is very much tied up with the presentation of place, culture, heritage or events, and these presentations could be said to take place on stages that are created out of the interaction between destinations or attractions and their staff and visitors. We could even say that the stages on which tourism takes place are created by the tourism industry itself, the media and the behaviour of tourists (Hannam and Knox, 2010). Baerenholdt *et al.* (2004: 51) tell us that:

Tourism possesses some unique analogies with dramaturgical performance. Firstly, the spaces and times of tourism are characterised by their symbolic function. Tourism is enacted within a certain symbolic framework that can be conformed to, transformed or transgressed. . . . Secondly, tourism usually takes place within bounded spaces; spaces that thereby are transformed into 'dramaturgical landscapes' for performing tourism. Thirdly, like dramaturgical performances many of those bounded tourist spaces are densely managed, regulated and controlled by people and institutions acting as playwrights, directors and stage crew.

Edensor (2001) takes the metaphor of performance further by casting tourists, marketeers, attraction staff and managers, and tour guides as the playwrights, directors and stage crew, as indicated in the above quotation. This extension of the metaphor gives us a sense of how each tourist encounter is the coming together of all aspects of a performance to create a whole, including an audience (Hannam and Knox, 2010).

In *The God of Small Things*, the novelist Arundhati Roy (1997) refers to the neo-colonial influence of contemporary tourism and its impacts upon local and regional culture such as the performance of all-night Kathakali dancing in which the original form of the dancing has evolved to accommodate the demands of Western tourists (Aitchison, 2001) (Figure 3.2). Originally, these performances were based on the Hindu epics such as the *Ramayana*, the *Mahabharata* and the *Puranas* and took place in the temple grounds during the night. Nowadays, these are staged as authentic experiences for tourists, with the timing and location arranged to suit the tourists' tastes. In this scenario, we might imagine Kerala Kathakali dancers at a tourist hotel in Kovalam performing their traditional cultural act and then returning backstage to remove their costumes and put on the jeans, t-shirts and sneakers they normally wear. The fact that the performance is an act rather than a simple exposure to the everyday life of a twenty-first-century Kerala life does not make the performance any less effective in restating something about Kerala culture. In MacCannell's (1973) original account, however, such staging or performing has negative connotations surrounding the idea of presenting pastiche or fake versions of a culture. We would argue that it need not necessarily be, however, that a fake version of anything is being performed, but

*Figure 3.2* Kathakali, Kerala.

merely that something else is taking place behind the scenes in order to preserve something of the spectacle of an attraction (Hannam and Knox, 2010; see also Chapter 4).

Indeed, dancing has been seen as a particularly interesting field of enquiry by social scientists concerned with the issue of embodied performances. Dance is a ritualised practice that has strong relationships to texts such as instruction manuals and rules and regulations. Primarily, however, dance is about physical movement and experience – it could be said to be extra-discursive in that dancing is very much about feeling, emotion and losing oneself to sensation (Malbon, 1999; Nash, 2000). This, as many commentators (Desmond, 1999; Nash, 2000; Thrift, 1997) have noted, makes it very difficult to satisfactorily describe or explain dance in writing. In his work on music, dance and tourism in Goa, Arun Saldanha (2002, 2005, 2007) attempts to do this through what he calls 'sensuous scholarship'. His work specifically examines the psychedelic rave culture in Goa:

> There are a few points I'd like you to remember about Anjuna's music tourism. First, on its own (even if we could think this), music is meaningless. The sounds mean because they're connected to a range of other entities and conditions: the sun, the moon, the temperature, the coconut trees, the rocks, the smells of kerosene and cannabis and sweat – all these are implicated in the Goa trance event. Second, the most important connection music makes is with human bodies. Bodies dancing, of course, but also selling, buying, sitting, deejaying, working. Different bodies have different relationships to the music, and move around the event in different ways. Third, Goa trance and trance in Goa are about the continuum of music and drugs.
>
> (Saldanha, 2002: 53)

Although, Goa is not experienced by every cultural tourist as in the account above, Saldanha's (2002, 2005) work does give us a pertinent example of the complexities involved in the embodied performance of a particular form of cultural tourism, this time by guests rather than hosts as in the Kerala example. His later work (Saldanha, 2007) also demonstrates the complex interplay between different groups of tourists in Goa where 'Goa freaks', backpackers, charter tourists, domestic tourists each know their place in the Goan visual economy but sometimes come into racial, sexual or bodily conflict with each other.

## Conclusions

The chapter has drawn upon the contemporary theoretical literature on cultural tourism and events to develop an examination of aspects of 'conventional' cultural tourism such as the 'arts', as in Bollywood film tourism, the contradictions of slum tours as a contested form of 'everyday' cultural tourism, and the ways in which dance is embodied and performed as a cultural tourism activity by both hosts and guests in India. Of course, this chapter links into further chapters such as Chapter 4 on heritage tourism and Chapter 5 on nature-based tourism. It also links up with the chapters on international tourism, domestic tourism and tourism mobilities.

# 4    Heritage tourism in India

## Introduction

This chapter critically examines the various contemporary conflicts over heritage interpretation and use in India. It draws upon recent academic theoretical discussions over the political contestation of heritage to facilitate a more nuanced discussion of India's monuments and museums, India's colonial heritage and some of India's World Heritage Sites, particularly the iconic Taj Mahal. Finally, we discuss the production and consumption of souvenirs in the Indian context. First, however, we examine contemporary theoretical discussions of heritage.

Heritage tourism clearly embraces a wide variety of different themes, including the analysis of museums, landscapes, artefacts and activities that concentrate on representing different aspects of the past (Graham *et al.*, 2000). Although heritage as a concept 'begins with the highly individualised notion of personal inheritance or bequest (e.g. through family wills and legacies)' (Johnson, 1999: 189–190), it is with respect to the 'imagined community' of nationhood that heritage is often most frequently connected (Anderson, 1983). This is particularly so in a country such as India, which consists of many different cultures and religions, and where an alleged common identity plays an important role for 'national' heritage development.

In addition to these issues, the heritage 'industry' is clearly a significant business these days, and every city, town and village seemingly needs to identify a number of historic monuments, museums, quarters or heritage trails in order to attract the tourism industry and, indeed, tourists (Hewison, 1987). Stories then need to be attached to these heritage sites in order to entertain or inform tourists once they have decided to make a visit to the location in question. If history is an academic pursuit concerned with uncovering the truths of the past, heritage is about the creative application of meaning and significance to sites in order to create historical touristic interest. Nevertheless, as Appadurai and Breckenridge (1999: 404) remind us, in India 'history and heritage are not yet [just] parts of a bygone past that is institutionalised in history books and museums'. Indeed, as we shall see in the Indian context, sometimes the relationships between history, archaeology and heritage are close and comfortable, but often they are somewhat more fractious as the very different goals of academic research and attracting tourists pull practitioners in different directions (Hannam and Knox, 2010).

The selection of which stories to tell about sites of apparent historical interest is always a political process within which experts and enthusiasts compete to have their opinions heard. Heritage landscapes are sometimes (re)created in the form of the past in order to achieve the political aim of signifying the values of the past in the present. Nevertheless, governments (and India is no exception to this) have quite consciously set out to bring back particular moral values into social life through the valorisation of certain types of heritage over others. As we shall see in our discussions below, the creation, then, of such forms of nostalgia is not simply a reflection of a latent human need for stability, but a much more politically contested form of collective remembering (Graham *et al.*, 2000; Johnson, 1999).

## India's museums and monuments

Historically, museums in India as modern institutions that we recognise today emerged largely during the colonial period (Appadurai and Breckenbridge, 1999). As Hermann Goetz noted:

> The museums started under British rule had been intended mainly for the preservation of the vestiges of a dying past, and only subsidiarily as a preparation for the future. Museums were the last haven of refuge for interesting architectural fragments, sculptures and inscriptions which saved them from the hands of an ignorant and indifferent public or from unscrupulous contractors who would have burned them to lime, sunk them into foundations or melted them down. Into the museums the products of the declining indigenous industries were accumulated, in the vain hope that they might serve as models for the inspiration of artisans and the public. Mineralogical, botanical, zoological and ethnological collections were likewise started, though rarely developed systematically; often they did not grow beyond sets of hunting trophies.
>
> (1954, cited in Appadurai and Breckenbridge, 1999: 407)

Perhaps as a consequence, until relatively recently many museums in India have been rather neglected and have not been invested in. Like many other touristic spaces in India, museums have thus had a rather ambivalent status. Appadurai and Breckenbridge (1999) contend that this is partly down to a number of cultural and historical factors, such as a living past focused on sacred places; the conjunction of the sacred with the everyday; and the embeddedness of people with their everyday environment (see also Chapter 7). More recently, however, museums in India have begun to have a greater public focus, in part because of the renewed interest in education but also because of the rise of the Indian middle classes and domestic tourism as well as the renewed ways in which India's museums have attempted to engage with the contemporary globalised world of tourism and leisure, albeit tentatively and implicitly. India's museums, it has been argued, 'look simultaneously in two directions' (Appadurai and Breckenbridge, 1999: 404). On the one hand, they seek to perform transnational ideologies of cosmopolitanism aimed at the Indian diaspora (see also Chapter 8) and, on the other, they are bound up with the recreation of frequently contested series of national heritage forms.

In terms of the latter, contemporary museums, in India as elsewhere, often claim to be politically neutral displays of regional or national cultures that tell the stories of those cultures to both domestic and international visitors. However, some objects are frequently selected for display while others are excluded, not just because a museum has too many exhibits to show but also in order to meet the (largely unwritten) political aims of the museum's benefactors (see Bennett, 1995; Graham *et al.*, 2000). For example, the National Museum in New Delhi predominantly displays objects that emphasise India's pre-colonial past as a past of unheralded civilisation and culture (see Box 4.1).

Another way in which landscapes are inscribed with a sense of the past is, of course, through monuments – statues and such like, usually of famous men and relating to 'heroic' acts. Again, these are relatively selective and often reflect political choices. In India there are, of course, many statues of Mahatma Gandhi – the 'father of India' – but also many others of various national and regional

---

**Box 4.1  National Museum, New Delhi**

The Archaeology unit in the National Museum has a prestigious collection of Indian sculptural art. There are about nine thousand art objects representing all major regions, schools and periods. It includes works carved in stone as well as terracottas, bronzes, stucco figures, gold, silver, bone and ivory images dated from the 3rd century B.C. to the 19th century A.D. Foyer & Corridor: The monumental image of Surya from the world famous Sun Temple of Konarak greets the visitor first. Eight pillars, surrounding the Surya image, present beautiful female figurines standing in different postures. While five of them belong to Mathura art (2nd cent. A.D.) the remaining three are the products of 10th–12th cent. A.D. Four railings pillars from Mathura carved with various damsels performing various functions are Khadganrtya, a lady taking bath under a spring. Ashokadohad and the mother carrying the child. The fifth one is Sri Lakshmi, the goddess of plenty and prosperity. Carved in marble, the statue of Jaina Saraswati from Pallu (Rajasthan) is a highly sophisticated and delicate work of sculptural art. She is the goddess of music, learning and intelligence. Alasakanya from Khajuraho region and the lady playing with ball from Nagda are other attractions. On either side of the reception counter, the visitor sees two well-known sculptures of Indian art – a superb image of Shiva in vamana form from Mansar (5th cent. A.D.) and a rare exhibit of the Yaksha from Pitalkhora, Maharashtra (2nd cent. B.C.) carved by a goldsmith, Kanhadasa, as is evident from the epigraph.

(http://www.nationalmuseumindia.gov.in/arch.html)

politicians who have served various causes, such as those that commemorate the *Dalit* or 'untouchable' leader B. R. Ambedkar. However, again these are frequently sites of political contestation.

The journalist Datta (2009) cites the sociologist Meera Kosambi as arguing that 'statuary is a colonial inheritance that serves little purpose. . . . If statues are to be erected, then (Ambedkar) is to, my mind, somebody really worth commemorating'. Datta (2009) argues that the desire to honour Ambedkar must be understood in the context of his 'contribution to the mobilisation of Dalits and giving them a pride in themselves'. She goes on to chart how:

> The depth of emotion invested in Ambedkar memorials explains the history of violence attached to them. Residents of Ghatkopar's Ramabai Nagar rioted in 1997 when they found that a statue of Ambedkar had been garlanded with slippers. In 2006, angry mobs burnt the Deccan Queen when an Ambedkar monument was desecrated in Kanpur. Only last week, a couple were in danger of being mobbed when they, allegedly, damaged a photograph of Ambedkar in Buddha Vihar, a Buddhist trust in Thane.

On the other hand, as we discuss below, many statues of British colonial leaders can be found in an unkept field in New Delhi, largely abandoned and forgotten as an act of colonial heritage erasure.

Whereas monuments are usually symbols of only one person or one ideal, war memorials and other commemorative landscapes such as cemeteries are there to commemorate many people or whole communities. War memorials can be seen as ways in which to commemorate those men and women who gave their lives for others, as well as the ideals of democracy, freedom and justice that attach to particular military campaigns. Nuala Johnson (1999) calls such memorials 'circuits of memory' through which the collective remembering of the nation can take place. Again we can see this in New Delhi at the India Gate or as it was formerly known the All-India War Memorial. This was built by the British to commemorate over 10,000 of the soldiers of the Indian Army who died during World War I and the subsequent wars in Afghanistan. However, some nostalgically complain that the site is now used more often as a place of leisure and tourism rather than as a place of remembrance (Delhimonuments.info, 2009).

## India's colonial heritage

India's heritage tourism is largely maintained by the semi-autonomous Archaeological Survey of India (ASI), which was originally established in 1861. Today it functions as a large and complex organisation 'attached' to the Department of Culture, in the Ministry of Tourism and Culture. Under the Ancient Monuments and Archaeological Sites and Remains Act of 1958, the ASI has declared over 3,000 monuments to be of national importance in India. The ASI's major activities have expanded to include the maintenance, conservation and preservation of protected monuments and sites, archaeological exploration and excavations, chemical preservation of monuments and antiquarian remains, architectural survey of monuments, the setting up and reorganisation of site museums, and the creation of greater awareness of the heritage of India (ASI, 2004). The ASI attempts to portray an all-India viewpoint independent of political bias; however, its independence has been questioned by the recent right-wing governments in India associated with the Bharatiya Janata Party (BJP). Indeed, the BJP has actively sought the Hinduisation of many archaeological sites and the renaming of many towns and cities. Moreover, at archaeological sites associated with India's colonial past, the representations have also taken on a nationalistic pedigree (Hannam, 2006).

For example, the so called 'British' Residency in Lucknow – site of one of the most (in)famous conflicts between the British colonists and the Indian population – remains to this day almost exactly as it was over 100 years ago as a monument to a colonial conflict (Figure 4.1). It was not erased, rebuilt or restored, but conserved by the ASI, the Indian National Trust for Archaeological and Cultural Heritage (INTACH) and the Uttar Pradesh State Tourism Department. The Residency site was declared a monument of British 'national' importance in 1920, but not opened to the general public until 1957, exactly 100 years after the conflict (K. G. Menon, 2003). However, recent interpretations of the conflict by the ASI have begun to reinscribe the site as a memorial to the Indian resistance rather than as a memorial to British domination.

*Figure 4.1* Residency, Lucknow.

In a recent ASI publication, K. G. Menon (2003: 5), the Director-General of the ASI, has argued that the ruins of the Residency 'stand as a mute witness to the intense resistance to domination by a foreign power'. Another recent ASI publication contains a message from the former Prime Minister of India, Vajpayee:

> The revolt of 1857 forms an important turning point in Indian history. It marked the beginning of India's First War of Independence, demonstrating the national feeling and action against alien rule in India. . . . The Residency at Lucknow which was built by Nawab Saadat Ali Khan for the use of the British Resident in 1800 is a mute witness to the dramatic events leading to its siege during the First War of Independence in 1857. Every brick of the Residency echoes with the sense of patriotism, sacrifice and heroic deeds of countless freedom fighters who lost their lives when it was besieged.
>
> (Fonia, 2002: 1)

The museum exhibits at the Residency, meanwhile, 'comprise an extensive range of material – from old photographs, lithographs, paintings and documents to artefacts and memorabilia, which invoke the high points of a revolt that has remained embedded in the collective memory of the people' (K. G. Menon, 2003: 5). The archaeologist in charge of the residency, Fonia (2002: 4) has similarly argued that 'It is our hope that each individual who walks into the galleries of this Museum will be able to re-live the spirit of [the] First War of Independence fought in and around Lucknow'. This reinterpretation of this archaeological site as one of Indian rather than British heritage was further demonstrated in 2007 when a group of British historians and ex-soldiers whose ancestors were involved in the historical conflict were forced to abandon a three-week tour of sites commemorating 150 years since the conflict after 'mobs' pelted them with mud and bottles (Ramesh, 2007). The trouble began within days of the group arriving after sections of the Indian media described their visit as a 'celebration of a British victory'. Muslim clerics and Hindu nationalists joined together to denounce the trip as an 'insult to Indian freedom fighters' (Ramesh, 2007).

However, we should also note that this is one of the few colonial-era heritage sites that is actively managed and preserved. The acclaimed travel writer William Dalrymple (1993: 110) has described the remains of the Residency in Old Delhi as follows:

> Although the mansion has survived virtually in its entirety, it has fallen on hard times. Rubbish and dirt spilled into the Residency compound from the fly-blown streets outside. Scaffolding propped up one side of the main facade. The space in front of the mansion . . . where the Resident's carriage would have jolted to a holt after audiences in the Red Fort – was left neglected by the civil servants who now occupied the building.

Of course, although Dalrymple's travelogue may be accused of romanticising India's colonial heritage, the point he makes is apt – as India forges its national identity very often it chooses to ignore its colonial heritage in favour of its more recently designated World Heritage Sites, which we discuss below.

## India's World Heritage Sites

Not only is India's colonial heritage revisited and contested, but also India's World Heritage Sites. Recently official government interpretations of India's colonial heritage sites have led to a renaming process. For example, in 2004 the World Heritage Site Victoria Terminus Station in Mumbai was renamed the Chhatrapati Shivaji Terminus. In this context the nomination process to become a World Heritage Site should be remembered. Following the adoption of the World Heritage Convention in 1972 (UNESCO, 1972), governments who signed the convention can propose sites of 'outstanding values' for world heritage listing. Possible sites include monuments, groups of buildings, natural sites and since 1992 cultural landscapes. Proposed sites are put on a national tentative list that is submitted to advising organisations such as the International Council of Monuments and Sites (ICOMOS) in the case of cultural heritage and the World Conservation Union (IUCN) in the case of natural sites. The 'outstanding values' refer to the natural, artistic, historic or architectural elements of the site. According to the regularly revised UNESCO guidelines (UNESCO, 2008a), the tentative sites have to meet at least one out of ten criteria (see Box 4.2). India has at the time of writing twenty-seven World Heritage Sites of which only five are natural sites, with the Manas Wildlife Sanctuary of Assam being on the List of World Heritage in Danger (see also Chapter 5).

Cultural World Heritage Sites in India are managed by the ASI, which is responsible for the protection, preservation and the valorisation of the sites. Another twenty-seven sites figure on the 'Tentative List', waiting to be listed. Of the twenty-seven listed sites, only two date from the colonial era, the Chhatrapati Shivaji Terminus and the Churches of Goa. All other sites are representative of former rulers (Hindu or Mughal dynasties) or are major religious archaeological sites representing one of the dominant religious groups of India. Indeed, India's tourism authorities promote the country to the outside world as being the birthplace of at least four different religions (Hinduism, Buddhism, Jainism and Sikhism) (Bandyopadhyay *et al.*, 2008; see also Chapter 7).

Yet, when we look closer at some of India's World Heritage Sites, such as the Red Fort, they are not only about important historic rulers, but also about national identity. Located in Old Delhi, the Red Fort is promoted by ASI as a symbol of the uprising against the British colony in 1857. After partition in 1947, it was in the Red Fort that independence was proclaimed by the raising of the Indian national flag on the top of the Fort. The site is therefore strongly linked symbolically to the creation of India's national identity.

Park (2010) divides national identity in relation to heritage into two groups: the 'modernistic perspective' and the 'primordial perspective'. Whereas the second one refers to antiquity of nations and the socio-cultural implications of ethnic ties, the modernistic perspective relates to the identification of nations as products

---

**Box 4.2  Criteria for inclusion on the list of World Heritage Sites (WHS)**

  i   to represent a masterpiece of human creative genius;
 ii   to exhibit an important interchange of human values, over a span of time or within a cultural area of the world, on developments in architecture or technology, monumental arts, town-planning or landscape design;
iii   to bear a unique or at least exceptional testimony to a cultural tradition or to a civilization which is living or which has disappeared;
 iv   to be an outstanding example of a type of building, architectural or technological ensemble or landscape which illustrates (a) significant stage(s) in human history;
  v   to be an outstanding example of a traditional human settlement, land-use, or sea-use which is representative of a culture (or cultures), or human interaction with the environment especially when it has become vulnerable under the impact of irreversible change;
 vi   to be directly or tangibly associated with events or living traditions, with ideas, or with beliefs, with artistic and literary works of outstanding universal significance. (The Committee considers that this criterion should preferably be used in conjunction with other criteria);
vii   to contain superlative natural phenomena or areas of exceptional natural beauty and aesthetic importance;
viii  to be outstanding examples representing major stages of earth's history, including the record of life, significant ongoing geological processes in the development of landforms, or significant geomorphic or physiographic features;
 ix   to be outstanding examples representing significant ongoing ecological and biological processes in the evolution and development of terrestrial, fresh water, coastal and marine ecosystems and communities of plants and animals;
  x   to contain the most important and significant natural habitats for in-situ conservation of biological diversity, including those containing threatened species *of outstanding universal value from the point of view of science or conservation.*

(UNESCO, 2008a)

---

of modern historical developments and processes (Park, 2010: 118). Indeed, the modern state of India has sought to reconstruct an Indian national identity that reaches beyond the numerous ethnic groups and religions that compose the country (Kakar, 2007). The recent increase in political tensions, most notably between Hindus and Muslims, is due in part to issues of global Islamophobia since 9/11, a situation that has impacted on India's domestic affairs with the November 2008 terrorist attacks in Mumbai. However, as we have seen above it is also linked to the *Hindutva* represented by the BJP. Indeed post-independence movements whose concept of the nation remains basically civic and territorial will seek to bring together and integrate into a new political community often disparate ethnic populations and to create a new 'territorial nation' out of the old colonial state.

(Smith, 1991: 82)

With this background, new management plans for how to interpret and present India's World Heritage Sites may become extremely relevant for the internal peace process.

Pretes's (2003) analysis of heritage sites as creators of a common identity or 'imagined community' among a diverse population can be enlarged to World Heritage Sites. One of the intentions of UNESCO is indeed that, all over the world, World Heritage Sites address an 'imagined community' encompassing national boundaries (Di Giovine, 2009). However, World Heritage Sites are also intended to foster national identity by promoting specific aspects of the nation's past. In general, World Heritage Sites are state owned and in that context heritage tourism can be seen as a specific discourse that is about 'sites and visions of nationhood they create reflecting the values and agenda of the owner and management organisations' (Palmer, 2005: 8).

The majority of the listings took place in the 1980s before the 'opening' of India and the burgeoning tourism development in the 1990s. The timing of most of the listings might be a reason why so few World Heritage Sites in India have a management plan and are protected. It was only in 1996 that UNESCO reformed the listing procedure by introducing a compulsory management plan as part of the application to become a World Heritage Site. In some cases, however, UNESCO pressures governments to work on a management plan before the site deteriorates. The management plan should position the site as an integral part of local and regional conservation and tourist and development plans, and not as 'intrusive islands of conservation'. Local involvement through stakeholders plays an important role for the site conservation and presentation strategies in such a plan. For instance, commercial activities benefiting the local community need to be organised, and top-down approaches and displacement of local residents avoided (Hampton, 2005).

For governments, the listing of World Heritage Sites is, along with the wish for preservation of the site, connected to the idea that the place will draw numerous visitors and possibly help to further develop a place or even an entire region. Yet it is not really clear how far a listing actually impacts on visitor numbers. Very little research exists and the results leave space for both options. For Shackley (1998), Hall and Piggin (2001) and Buckley (2004) the nomination is influencing visitor numbers positively. On the other hand, Cohen (2008) argues that listing has little impact on motivations to visit a site. For Cohen, visitor increase is more due to concerted marketing campaigns after the designation rather than simply because of the listing.

If World Heritage Sites are pull factors for a country, this has implications for the wider management of infrastructures, transport, shops, etc. beyond the site itself (Shackley, 1998). Compulsory buffer zones in India are mostly non-existent and tourism development in the forms of stalls and shops selling souvenirs goes as far as the ticket booths of the sites. In any case, visitor management needs or should be an integral part of any management plan. This includes issues such as physical protection, presentation and interpretation, all almost entirely absent at India's World Heritage Sites. At most sites visitors can freely walk and touch elements of the site; fragile carvings and sculptures are exposed and walked on as shown in Figure 4.2. Visitors climb on statues and relax on parts of the heritage. Little in the way of signage or surveillance hinders them in doing so. Listing a site for its 'outstanding value' implies that information will be provided to the

*Figure 4.2* Boy climbing on World Heritage Site.

visitors. Unfortunately, neither presentation nor interpretation is very frequent at India's World Heritage Sites and often the level of on-site interpretation is very basic (Shackley, 1998: 7).

Visitors who wish to learn more about a site need to rely for explanations on self-declared guides or guidebooks. Most sites have a little booklet with a minimum of information sold by the sellers in front of the site. The near absence of official material presenting and helping to understand a heritage site, such as its significance for history, architecture or culture, or even as world heritage, stands in opposition to the wish by authorities to bring visitors to the site and boost development. This lack of information often leaves many Western visitors frustrated or annoyed for they feel hassled by the numerous self-declared guides proposing their services. But the stereotypical approaches of UNESCO heritage management plans translate Western attitudes towards heritage and do not necessarily correspond to the local (or national) cultural understanding of a site.

Indeed, different visitor groups expect and use heritage sites differently. Although everybody agrees on the 'outstanding values' of the place, interpretations can be varying and are influenced by the origins, education and experiences of the visitor (Edensor, 1998). Whereas foreign visitors visit sites for architectural, artistic, aesthetic or historical reasons, domestic visitors often benefit from the sites for recreational reasons such as picnicking or taking a walk. For them a site is part of their environment and their identity and they are not particularly interested in the various aspects that attract foreign visitors. A recent survey by Mathy (2010) at the Red Fort in Delhi evidenced the different perceptions of the presentation of a World Heritage Site by locals and by foreign visitors. Whereas the local visitor came for recreation and appreciated the on-site museum, foreign visitors criticised the lack of interpretation and old-fashioned displays and expressed that it was a disappointing experience.

Nevertheless, the ASI has recently prepared some management plans for the most visited World Heritage Sites in India, such as the Red Fort and the Elephanta Caves. For instance, the Red Fort, which was in the hands of the Indian army until 2003, has had a management plan since March 2009 drafted by the ASI and the Cultural Resource Conservation Initiative (ASI and CRCI, 2009). Besides the aforementioned significance of the Fort for the Indian nation, the plan outlines how the future interpretation will be developed. It should be noted that only the Mughal buildings are protected under the Ancient Monuments and Archeological Sites and Remains Act 1958; the colonial buildings are not (ASI and CRCI, 2009: 2). We can see the problems involved in caring for India's World Heritage Sites more deeply by examining the iconic Taj Mahal.

## The Taj Mahal

In contrast, the Taj Mahal, as one of the most emblematic and symbolic sites of India, has not yet an integrated management plan. Indeed, the Taj plays a very particular role in the tourism and heritage landscape of India. The mausoleum of white marble was built in Agra between 1631 and 1653 by order of the Mughal

Indian emperor Shah Jahan in memory of his favourite wife and is indeed one of the most renowned World Heritage Sites both within and outside India. Listed in 1983, according to the inscription on the UNESCO world heritage list, 'the Taj Mahal is the jewel of Muslim art in India and one of the universally admired masterpieces of the world's heritage' (UNESCO, 2008b). Edensor (2004: 103) writes of a 'truly global icon used to conjure up notions of planetary unity and diversity'. He also observed in his seminal work on the Taj the variety of 'imaginaries' linked to the Taj by the different communities and their subsequent interpretations. For the Muslim community the site represents tombs of Sufi saints, whereas for Western tourists the site is connected to romanticism (Edensor, 1998). In any case, the Taj is at the top of the 'must see' list for foreign as well as domestic visitors. It constitutes one of the points of the 'golden triangle' (see the section on Rajasthan below), comprising one of the most popular tourism areas in India (see also Chapter 2; Capella-Cervera and Priestley, 2008; Berger, 2008).

Most visitors come to Agra only for the Taj and disregard the other heritage sites, in particular the Agra Fort, which is also a World Heritage Site but lacks the emblematic signification of the Taj. This focus on the Taj is, according to Capella-Cervera and Priestley (2008: 83), due to 'a lack of sensibility and awareness from the public and the private decision makers in India'. For that reason, the city of Agra does not benefit from the masses of tourists arriving daily on the express train from Delhi, who visit the Taj, stay for one night and head back to Delhi. Hence, in order to counter the degradation as well as lengthen the stay of tourists for local benefit, new policies have been created. The ASI and the Agra Development Authorities decided to take measures aimed at reducing all of these negative impacts in 2000. The first measures taken were restrictions on opening. Until 2000 the Taj Mahal was open 24/7, with visitors occupying the site and surroundings in a disorganised manner. Opening hours were then introduced and openings for sunset and dawn limited to once a month.

As in many other countries, India makes a clear distinction between domestic and foreign visitors, and the entrance pricing policy has become a tool for visitor flow regulation and the protection of the site. However, this dual pricing policy led initially to open conflicts between Western tourists and the authorities managing the site. At present (2010) domestic tourists (including NRIs) pay Rs 20, whereas foreign tourists pay Rs 750. Included in this price is a bottle of water, the use of restrooms and slippers. Indians have to pay for restrooms (Rs 2) and slippers (Rs 20) with a resulting clear segmentation of domestic and foreign tourists on site. Almost all Indian visitors walk barefoot as access to the mausoleum is not allowed in shoes, whereas all foreign tourists wear white slippers. At weekends, in particular, there are long queues for domestic visitors.

The presence of 2.5 million tourists attracted local entrepreneurs to open restaurants, souvenir shops and hotels or hostels in the area immediately surrounding the site. The unplanned area around the Taj has been modified with the new policies and most of these places have closed down, pushing, in particular, the backpacker market out as prices are perceived to be too high (Edensor, 2004; see also Chapter 6). The Taj Mahal Cultural Heritage District Development Plan drafted by the American Society of Landscape Architects in 2002 aimed to create a link between the Agra Fort and the Taj through the 'rebuilding' of Mughal gardens between the two sites. It sought to integrate the Taj and Agra Fort in one big heritage 'park'. However, this plan is not an official world heritage management plan integrating the various aspects of local community involvement, site conservation and interpretation issues. Although the plan still has not been realised it was an interesting attempt to further commodify the site into more of an organised heritage theme park.

Although litter bins have been placed in the site and at the entrance, the site is still not clean, for these litter bins are hardly maintained. Drastic measures have been taken in relation to car emissions, with cars forbidden within 500 m of the site. A parking lot has been built on the outskirts of the site (about 15 minutes' walk) where visitors have to leave their cars and coaches. Electric buses then take them from the parking site to the main entrance. Because of the heat, many Western visitors tend to use the free shuttle service and as a consequence many of the small shops and restaurants along the road leading to the entrance have lost a lot of their potential clientele and risk economic decline. No official guided tour is available; rather, in an uncontrolled way self-declared guides propose tours to visitors. The scene showing the guided tour of the Taj by the protagonist in the film *Slumdog Millionaire* gives a witty example of the lack of control at the Taj, but is also representative of most heritage sites in India.

## Rajasthan

For many heritage tourists, Rajasthan is another 'must see' destination (Figure 4.3). It is a place promoted as the 'authentic and real' India, but, of course, many of these authentic traditions have been constructed as a result of colonial encounters (Henderson and Weisgrau, 2007) and can be linked back to the aforementioned orientalist constructions of India. Jaipur in Rajasthan, along with Agra and Delhi, form the so-called 'golden triangle' of places to visit. Tourist authorities and guidebooks promote this triangle as the perfect first, short contact with India (Berger, 2008). Figures from the Ministry of Tourism in 2008 show nearly 1.5 million foreign tourists and nearly 3 million domestic tourists visiting the state of Rajasthan (Ministry of Tourism, 2009a: 12–13). The state is widely perceived as a 'colourful' destination, with impressive heritage sites, palaces and sand dunes. More than any other state in India, heritage in Rajasthan is continually being recreated and performed as a product in response to the specific needs of actual or potential users (Tunbridge and Ashworth, 1996; Hardgrove, 2007). Given this, Henderson and Weisgrau (2007: xxx) in their analysis of tourism development in Rajasthan note that:

> Tourism discourse transforms Rajasthan from the poverty-stricken state lagging in most socioeconomic indicators in economic development reporting, into a colourful panorama of ancient customs, romantic history, peoples, and monuments. The state's economic and social progress, such as new

*Figure 4.3* Rajasthan tourism.

industries, urban development, and entrepreneurship, are edited out of the tourist encounter, as is the rural reality.

Furthermore, with reference to the dominant image of the Rajput princes, Bautès (2006: 182) states that it is:

> the process of recognition that favours their participation in the tourist economy for the culture of this group (Rajputs) and the image of the maharajas they represent, nourish to a certain extent the urban communities and their territorial identification, and more largely with Rajasthan.

Marketed and promoted as the land of the Maharajas, numerous palaces have been restored as luxury hotels to nourish the romantic, orientalist and 'exotic' imaginary for both domestic and foreign markets. These upmarket hotels address the wealthy domestic and international clientele with high prices comparable with Western rates and also the average rates in other Indian destinations (see Chapter 6). With increasing wealth in India and notably within the 'new' middle class, increasing numbers of domestic tourists are heading to Rajasthan for weekend trips to these luxury hotels (see also Chapter 7). Although some of these hotels belong to the large Indian hotel chains such as the Taj (e.g. the White Palace in

Udaipur), many others are privately owned by the families of former Maharajas. In Jodhpur, for example, travellers can stay in the luxurious palace of the Maharaja of Jodhpur built at the beginning of the twentieth century, which still houses his family. Such hotel palaces are also used for the weddings of the rich and famous, boosting and promoting this romantic and timeless staged image of Rajasthan nationally and internationally. The Maharaja of Jodhpur – Gaj Singh II – has been a key actor in this process. He is a symbol of success with close links not only to Rajasthan's heritage as one of the descendants of a royal family, but also to national and international visitors and business partners (Jhala, 2007). He thus benefits from tourism both through his present palace being partially transformed into a hotel and through his former palace in the city centre being a major heritage attraction. Hence, the combination of heritage hotels and heritage attractions commodifies the whole of Rajasthan into a staged fairytale land that draws upon orientalist imagery which evokes narratives of seventeenth-, eighteenth- and nineteenth-century India.

Another key example of this presentation of Rajasthan as an oriental imaginary is the state-owned Palace on Wheels luxury trains – a reconstitution of nineteenth-century trains – which now connect the significant heritage sites in the state. In contrast to our discussion of slum tourism in Chapter 3, in Rajasthan contemporary socio-cultural references to the local populations and cultures are voluntarily left aside (Henderson and Weisgrau, 2007) for the maintenance of the state's image as a site of luxury tourism (see Box 4.3).

Nevertheless, even though it owns the Palace on Wheels, the Rajasthan Tourism Development Corporation (RTDC) suffers from competition with the private sector (Rathore *et al.*, 2010). For instance, while private site owners invest in audio guides, state-owned sites are unable to provide much in the way of

---

**Box 4.3  The Palace on Wheels**

Climb aboard the legendary *Palace on Wheels* train for a week-long odyssey recreating the ambiance and glorious past as you travel through the heart of Rajasthan. You will feel like royalty on board one of the top ten luxury trains in the world as you visit little-seen and well-known attractions, including the famous Taj Mahal.

Welcome aboard the *Palace on Wheels* on its splendid and enchanting royal rail journey through the bygone era of the erstwhile Maharajas. Though times have changed and the winds have shifted, the *Palace On Wheels* cruises along in royal style, the kind only the Maharajas of yesteryears could have perpetuated and enjoyed.

The exquisite and exclusive *Palace On Wheels* has luxurious cabins, wall to wall carpeting, a well stocked bar, two dining cars and very personalized service . . . in fact, almost everything that could promise heaven on earth for seven days!

(http://palacetours.net/Tourview.aspx?tag=t1&tid=2)

interpretation, thus leaving visitors to their own devices in terms of interpretation. For example, in Jodhpur, the Maharaja Gaj Singh II opens his former palace for visitors and provides an audio guide with a personal welcome as well as testimonies from his wife about life in the former days of the palace and a detailed description of the architecture of the palace, taking the visitor around in a very personalised way and generating a positive experience for visitors. In contrast some publicly owned sites emphasise heritage performance in place of interpretation. One example is the pink palace or Hawa Mahal in Jaipur, the 'pink city'. Guards here are dressed up in historical clothes, sustaining the romantic imagery of the state. In 2008, the Rajasthan government assigned local dancers to entertain tourists visiting the Amber Fort. In order to complete the chosen image, performing arts are equally commodified to fit into the general context of recreated reality. For instance, the Bhats, a untouchable caste of singers and actors who formerly performed 'local myths and legends for Rajasthani merchants and military officers who had migrated to Delhi, Calcutta and Mumbai' (Snodgrass, 2007: 109), are nowadays performing puppet plays for foreign tourists in hotel lobbies and restaurants in Rajasthan.

Another widely promoted tourist experience in Rajasthan is elephant rides, which are, again, marketed explicitly as a 'royal experience'. The website http://rajasthantourstravel.com, for example, states that:

> In fact in the olden days when the Elephant was the royal carrier, the dignitaries and other guests of the royalty always rode up the winding path to the fort on Elephant back. The same experience has been recreated for tourists.

Another website, http://www.jaipur.org.uk/, declares that 'the best part of this tourist attraction . . . is the royal elephant ride'. However, in 2008 animal protection groups asked for a ban on these elephant rides following accidents involving visitors, but also because the elephants were allegedly being badly treated (*Times of India*, 25 August 2009). Yet demand from tourists has meant that elephants have had to be 'imported' from Bihar and Assam. A petition in August 2009 to stop the elephant rides did not get much support and elephants are still operating (see also Chapter 5). Rajasthan is also a site for the production and consumption of many souvenirs of India and it is to this topic that we now turn.

## Souvenirs of India

In his book *Shopping Tourism, Retail and Leisure* Dallen Timothy (2005) has charted the origins and meanings of souvenirs in the contemporary global economy. He notes that some of the earliest accounts of souvenirs date back to the Egyptians, but these were subsequently followed by many colonial explorers who 'acquired' by fair means and foul the arts and crafts of many of the indigenous peoples they encountered. Moreover, he also notes that many 'accepted' kinds of souvenirs are those associated with religious pilgrimages (see also Chapter 7). Today, souvenir purchasing is a major component of the global tourism industry and functions as a means for the tourist to literally 'remember' their experience of a place. Gordon (1986: 140–144) has developed a typology of five kinds of souvenirs, which is a useful starting point for our discussion of souvenirs in India:

Pictorial souvenirs such as postcards, photographs, posters and books.

'Piece-of-rock' souvenirs that are literally parts of the destination environment, such as a pebble from a beach.

Symbolic souvenirs that are manufactured items that conjure up thoughts about the place in which they were purchased, such as replicas of monuments.

Marked souvenirs that are inscribed with words or logos that mark a destination in place and/or time, such as an inscribed mug or other utility object.

Locally produced souvenirs that are indicative of local merchandise such as regional clothing and handicrafts.

Timothy (2005) adds a further sixth type of souvenir to this list called the situational souvenir, which refers to souvenirs of wars and disasters that may become valuable traveller possessions immediately following a devastating event and which may subsequently become very collectable, memorable and useful as elements of cultural capital for the discerning tourist as the event itself becomes commodified and passes into history. Indeed, such souvenirs can also become politicised, particularly if they have religious sentiments such as a souvenir of or from a contested monument (see our discussion above). Stanley (2000) thus argues that many tourists are akin to the earlier colonialists in their pursuit of souvenirs.

Moreover, it has often been argued that the inauthenticity of much heritage tourism often stems from the commodification processes that give a phenomenon an alienating and explicit exchange value (Watson and Kopachevsky, 1994; Rao and Suresh, 2001). According to this perspective, aspects of heritage tourism may also lead to a standardisation of culture and a translation of local phenomena into global culture, particularly through the production of souvenirs. On the other hand, aspects of heritage tourism may also lead to a revalorisation of a local culture as local people (re)develop their community though the production of souvenirs.

In looking for authenticity, some tourists focus on the product in terms of its uniqueness and originality, its workmanship, its cultural and historical integrity, its aesthetics and/or its functions and use. Interestingly, academic expertise may also be used to confer authenticity. Even a sense of place can confer a sense of authenticity – because something is sold in an 'authenticated' place it gives it added authenticity (Shenhav-Keller, 1993). Shopping at places where goods are actually made can even become a verification of the authenticity process – authenticity is conferred when the object is seen to have been made (Littrell *et al.*, 1993). Labels are also often placed on goods to make them seem more authentic, add a quality assurance tag and even explain their wider context. Such 'marking' helps to make explicit the exchange value of the product. But quite clearly the production of souvenir commodities can be a 'mixed blessing', because, although it may be lucrative for a host community, it may also lead to a craft product being mass produced and becoming inauthentic and disassociated from its original meaning. We can find these processes operating in many places in India.

Indeed, India is, of course, replete with souvenir shops, both small and large, aimed at both domestic and international tourists. Many of these contain pictorial and marked souvenirs as well as mass-produced symbolic souvenirs that are replicas of the major tourist sites of India, such as the Taj Mahal. In terms of locally produced souvenirs many of the shops seem to contain locally made products from only two dominant Indian states, namely Rajasthan and Kashmir. Products such as carpets and fabrics from these states fill the souvenir shops throughout the country, fostering the impression of an industrialised souvenir market. According to a survey of foreign tourist's expenditure on handicraft souvenirs, on average a foreign tourist spends about Rs 12,000 on handicraft souvenirs, with female tourists spending more than their male counterparts (National Productivity Council, 2002). This is estimated to be worth nearly Rs 30 million per annum to the Indian economy. Interestingly, this survey notes that silk products had the highest expenditure per tourist, followed by metal and jewellery, cotton and wool textiles and leather products. The Indian government is clearly hugely aware of the importance of the souvenir market with the recent establishment of new Cottage Industries Emporiums outside New Delhi that seek to bring together regionally produced souvenirs within an air-conditioned environment aimed at international and diaspora tourists (see Box 4.4).

Moreover, aware of the globalisation of the souvenir product and the fact that visitors spend less money in the absence of identified local products, the Ministry of Tourism in the state of Kerala decided in 2009 to reintroduce unique and 'authentic' local artefacts as souvenirs. A selection of forty-seven specific items has been submitted to tour operators for them to choose around thirty popular souvenirs that will be produced locally and thus benefit the local population while creating and reinforcing a chosen image of Kerala (*The Hindu*, 22 January 2009).

Another example of local souvenir production and consumption can be seen at Mamallapuram (formerly Mahabalipuram), a town founded by the Pallava kings, which was carved out of rock along the Coromandel coast south of Chennai in the seventh and eighth centuries (Figure 4.4). This town has become well known, especially since its 1985 World Heritage Site designation for its *rathas* (temples in the form of chariots), *mandapas* (cave sanctuaries), giant open-air reliefs such as the famous 'Descent of the Ganges', and the temple of Rivage, with thousands of sculptures to the Hindu god Shiva. It is also a place where tourists awake to the sound of present-day rock carving, as local stonemasons make souvenirs of all sizes for the watching tourists. The extent to which this heritage site has been

---

**Box 4.4 The Central Cottage Industries Emporium**

The Central Cottage Industries Emporium serves as an air-conditioned environment where both domestic and international tourists can browse and purchase without haggling a variety of selected Indian crafts and souvenirs. Its website claims that:

> The cottage has been India's window to the World nearly over 50 years. The emporium has attracted a number of heads of States, Prime Ministers, Ambassadors, a host of other dignitaries from across the globe What began as an endeavour to preserve the traditional crafts-manship and excellence of skill as a part of national heritage has now become a cultural movement in its own way. It has brought about togetherness in all the various forms of arts, crafts and apparel of India under one roof. From a tiny sales depot the emporium has now been developed into the largest single emporium in the Country with extensive reputation and a stamp of ethnicity, authenticity and quality on all the merchandise it shelters. Come & discover the magic of India through the eyes of the Cottage.
>
> Envisaged as a showcase of the creations of Indian craftsmen, weavers and folk artists the Central Cottage Industries Emporium has been a favourite with customers in India and the World over. It has taken special care to make sure that you get a feel of what the real India is all about through its products the décor the exhibition and everything else that goes with it. This unique store has tackled Handicrafts sales on a multilateral front embracing market research, hand picked buying, imaginative promotion design development, impeccable merchandise, careful inventories and variety of auxiliary services to make it a complete shopping experience.
>
> (http://www.cottageemporium.in/corporate-info.html)

---

commodified is evident in the rather uncritical and unreflective description provided by the *Lonely Planet* guide to India:

> Mamallapuram is a tossed salad: ancient archaeological wonders, a fine, if windy strip of sand, good biryani in local dhabas (snack bars) and cheap internet in the traveller ghetto, one of the few in Tamil Nadu. . . . Bob Marley flags hang from balconies. Stores sell things from Tibet, 'Indian' clothes that few Indians would probably ever wear, toilet paper, hand sanitiser and used books, and you know you have landed, once again, in the Kingdom of Backpackistan.
>
> (S. Singh, 2009a: 1059)

Indeed the souvenir industry (local or not) has begun to take over the whole site, selling itself as the continuum of the temple carvers.

*Figure 4.4* Mamallapuram souvenirs.

## Conclusions

This chapter has critically examined the various contemporary conflicts over heritage interpretation and use in India. It has drawn upon recent academic theoretical discussions over the political contestation of heritage to facilitate a more nuanced discussion of India's monuments and museums, India's colonial heritage and some of India's World Heritage Sites, particularly the iconic Taj Mahal. Finally, we have discussed the production and consumption of souvenirs in the Indian context. The next chapter considers India's natural heritage as a contested tourism resource.

# 5    Nature-based tourism in India

## Introduction

This chapter critically examines the various contemporary conflicts involved in the use and management of nature-based tourism in India. It draws theoretically upon concepts of ecotourism and carrying capacity, ethics and community development to inform a discussion of these conflicts. Examples are drawn from some of the major national parks in India to illustrate these issues and conflicts (Hannam, 2005b). In so doing we wish to take a political ecology perspective in analysing the relationships between tourism and the environment in India. Blaikie and Brookfield (1987: 17) argue that a Third World political ecology combines the 'concerns of ecology and a broadly defined political economy'. Contemporary political ecologists have examined the politics of environmental change in the developing world in terms of certain problems, concepts, socio-economic characteristics and regions, or used a combination of these (Bryant, 1992; Peet and Watts, 1996; Bryant and Bailey, 1997; Peluso and Watts, 2001). Furthermore, Bryant and Bailey (1997: 3) point out that:

> Political ecologists appear to agree on two basic points. . . . Firstly, they agree that the environmental problems facing the Third World are not simply a reflection of policy or market failures . . . but rather are a manifestation of broader political and economic forces. . . . [A] second area of agreement among political ecologists is the need for far-reaching changes to local, regional and global political-economic processes.

Political ecologists are thus sceptical of the merits of concepts such as sustainable development, partly because of the way that such ideas have become swiftly incorporated into the dominant discourses of global organisations, nation-states and multi-national corporations without much change at the grassroots level. This is all the more apparent in developing world contexts in which the colonial legacy of commodification and land degradation has led to the continuation of social and environmental conflicts in the post-colonial era. Ultimately, a political ecology approach is grounded in a historical and material analysis of the often complex and unequal relations of power within any environmental context. Critical political ecology perspectives then 'evaluate the dynamics of material and discursive struggles over natural resources, entitlements and power' (Gossling, 2003: 1) in various contexts. We believe that such a critical approach can be a powerful tool in understanding tourism–environment conflicts. First, then, we wish to conceptualise nature within the Indian context by drawing upon narratives from the historical colonial period.

## Nature and tourism in colonial India

In taking a political ecology approach to study the relations between tourism and nature in India, we need to examine first the historical colonial encounter whereby Western scientific conceptualisations of nature engaged with indigenous Indian environments in complex ways both positively and negatively. The dominant Western views of nature and the environment in general have been heavily influenced by various scientific interpretations, which have gained an immeasurable degree of cultural authority over the past 300 years. The development of Western scientific knowledge was also given impetus because of the so-called 'voyages of discovery' whereby Columbus, Cook and other explorers began to map the world. In so doing they brought back to the West new products and ideas about the natural world. However, this process of 'discovery' that underpinned new forms of travel also led more spectacularly to the transformation of both Western perspectives on nature and nature itself as these explorers also (sometimes unwittingly) took with them various animals and plants and agricultural methods to these countries that they 'discovered'.

Alfred Crosby (2004), for example, in his seminal thesis of ecological imperialism argued that the processes by which Europeans conquered the Americas and Australasia were not just military, technological and economic but also ecological – the introduction of plants, animals and microbes from Europe, which destroyed and replaced indigenous plants, animals and microbes. However, in his account of the biological expansion of Europe, Crosby (2004) only briefly dealt with the complex civilisations of China, India and the Middle East, which were, as he put it, 'within the reach' but 'beyond the grasp' of Europe (Grove, 1996). He argued that such factors as population densities, resistance to disease, agricultural technology and sophisticated socio-political organisations all made these areas more resistant to the ecological imperialism of Europe. Europeans may have been able to conquer the tropics but they were not able to Europeanise the tropics to the extent that they did in the Americas and Australasia – until, perhaps, more recently. This does not mean that European colonialism had an insignificant impact on tropical ecosystems. In India, for example, Europeans did not create a 'new world' by decimating the indigenous populations and their natural resource base, but they did intervene politically and radically alter existing food production systems and their ecological basis.

However, in his seminal book *Green Imperialism*, Richard Grove (1996:

382–383) has argued that in the first half of the nineteenth century the British contact with India's environment led to the seeds of modern conservation:

> In India the relative influence of scientists, and especially medical surgeons, in their relations with the colonial state became far more developed and the conservation propaganda they wielded more sophisticated. As experts consulted by government, the surgeons were incorporated in an entirely new kind of scientific civil service, in a structure that guaranteed some continuity in analysis and ensured that forest conservation was taken on by the state in India as an accepted part of the role of colonial government.

However, by the late nineteenth century, this conservationist impulse needs to be seen in a wider context:

> There is no doubt that environmental sensibilities in Britain, for example, were among some groups, almost as well developed by the 1860s as they were among the scientific services in India. They were very different kinds of sensibilities, however, and were associated with different kinds of social critique. The biota of Europe were simply not perceived as being threatened by rapid ecological change of the kind that was taking place in India. As a result, embryonic worries about the destruction of rural landscapes and about species extinctions remained the concern of a largely ineffective minority.
>
> (Grove, 1996: 462–463)

Nevertheless, by exposing the Indian environment and population to industrialisation and consumerisation the British in India ensured that these processes of ecological change would continue and even intensify after they left.

This provides a background to the developments in nature-based leisure and tourism during this period. In colonial India, travel and recreation in what became India's national parks and protected areas were largely the preserve of the British elite for the purposes of hunting (MacKenzie, 1988; Hannam, 2008). For example, although hunting and killing tigers had been a sport of the earlier Mughal rulers of India, with the onset of colonialism it became a much more widespread leisure/tourism pursuit for the colonial elite (Pandian, 2001). Although shooting tigers was primarily a leisure practice, many Western visitors came to India to visit friends and relatives and engaged in the 'sport' of tiger shooting as part and parcel of their tour. During the colonial period, India was run by a relatively small number of highly trained civil servants, military officers, police officers and forest officers (Cohn, 1983, 1987). These men wielded considerable individual power and would commonly spend their whole lives in India. As such they generated a particular way of life that outside office hours centred primarily on *shikar* (the Hindi term for hunting), in particular shooting tigers. As MacKenzie (1988: 180) has argued, 'The British and the tiger seemed in some ways to be locked in conflict for command of the Indian environment'. Indeed a vast number of memoirs were published on the subject of *shikar* from the early 1800s, right up until Indian independence. The view from Colonel Glasfurd was that 'Few subjects of such comparatively circumscribed bounds have elicited more literature than has Indian sport' (Glasfurd, 1905: v, cited in MacKenzie, 1988: 168).

Titles such as 'Silver Hackle's' (1929) *Indian Jungle Lore and the Rifle*, Sanderson's (1878) *Thirteen Years among the Wild Beasts of India*, Stebbing's (1911) *Jungle By-Ways in India*, Aitken's (1897) *A Naturalist on the Prowl or in the Jungle* and Glasfurd's (1928) *Musings of an Old Shikari* tend to give the impression that hunting was merely an escape from the routine pressures of administration. However, hunting in India was also essential to the reproduction of the British colonial state in India. More specifically hunting tigers was emblematic of the exercise of colonial state power and reinforced both the claim to rule and the aura of British invincibility – the sense that the British colonial state was so powerful that it was useless to oppose it. In addition, through shooting tigers the British also enhanced the sense of the benevolent state: getting rid of the man-eating tiger fed into the notion that the British were modernising and taming nature for the benefit of the Indian population (see Corbett, 1944).

Beyond the rather glib assertions that hunting was simply something to do to either relieve the boredom or gain a decorative trophy, many other British hunters centred their arguments about their reasons for hunting around constructions of an aggressive masculine sense of British identity, which conversely, of course, excluded other competing definitions of both masculinity and nationhood. This late Victorian manliness emphasised the ideal of a virile, muscular and patriotic sense of endurance above all (see Mangan and Walvin, 1987; Phillips, 1997; Hannam, 2008).

First, tiger shooting was seen as a quintessentially British thing to do. This can be seen in the following quotations. Best (1931: xii–xiii) commented that:

> Every man is by nature a hunter, and more particularly the average young Englishman; sport of some sort can be found anywhere, provided one has the keenness to look for it, and the knowledge of how to look; even a rat or a squirrel provides some interest and experience in its chase.

Dunlop (1860: 2), meanwhile, agreed that:

> It has been said, that hunting instincts more or less pervade all nature, but Anglo-Saxons are the only true sportsmen in the world: and, in the case of English gentlemen, there is no doubt but that instinct and habit, alternatively cause and effect, do much in producing that activity, and energy of mind and body, that promptitude in danger, and passion for fair play which they carry with them wherever they wander.

Hunting was thus seen as an instinctual part of the British national character – a character that was caught up in an ethical tradition of British fair play and sportsmanship. Brown (1887: 278) similarly noted that: 'It has often been a matter of surprise to me that British sportsmen, with the means to gratify the love of sport that is inherent in most Englishmen, do not oftener go in for a *shikar* trip to the sunny land of the East'. Brown argued at length that hunting should be pursued in India both because it was much cheaper than in other parts of the British Empire and because servants, transport and medical aid were more easily procured in India. However, interestingly he concluded that hunting in India was much better than elsewhere because the British sportsman in India knew 'that, as one of dominant race, his wishes will be more likely to be forwarded by the native inhabitants, than they would be in any other part of the world' (Brown, 1887: 278).

The sites of colonial hunting and recreation would become the national parks of India after independence (Hannam, 2008). Many areas of the world have modelled their protection system on the late nineteenth-century US national parks system. The US Congress decreed that these national parks would serve as 'pleasure grounds' for visitors, thus linking national parks to tourism from the start. Other countries followed suit: Australia (1879), Mexico (1898), Argentina (1903) and Sweden (1909) (see Eagles and McCool, 2002). Moreover, many national parks around the world have become 'cited' as being of World Heritage status (see also Chapter 4). However, much of the land that has subsequently been protected or conserved as national parks in *non-Western* countries was originally primarily conserved as hunting areas for the British colonial elite rather than for the ostensibly more noble concerns of conserving nature.

The first national park to be created in India was Corbett in 1936. Since independence a network of eighty-nine national parks, together with some 500 smaller wildlife sanctuaries, has been developed (Ministry of Environment and Forests, 2003). Below we discuss the complex post-independence relations and conflicts between forestry management, national park management and nature-based tourism management in India.

## Tourism, forestry and national parks in contemporary India

Forestry and forest management also has a much longer history than tourism management in India and much historical research has been undertaken in this area (see Jewitt, 1995; Rangarajan 1996; Sivaramakrishnan 1999; Skaria 1999; Hannam, 1999, 2004a). By 1894 most of the natural forested areas of India came under strict management control as either 'reserved' or 'protected'. In the former category of forests local rights were commuted, whereas in the latter category local rights were regulated. National parks fell into the first category (Sagreiya, 1967).

In the post-colonial period, forests have also been reclassified into 'protection forests' needed for ecological reasons, 'national forests' needed for economic reasons and 'village forests' required by local people for subsistence. The last have since been developed through contested processes of 'joint forest management', which aims to actively involve local communities in the conservation and use of forest areas in India (Sunder, 2000; Sekher, 2001; Ballabh *et al.*, 2002; Kumar, 2002). National parks come under the category of 'protection forests' and constitute some 5 per cent of the entire country. It should be borne in mind that, although forestry contributes significantly to the Indian economy, the national parks are viewed primarily in terms of conservation. National parks in India come under the control of the Ministry of Environment and Forests, but since the mid-1990s the Ministry of Tourism has also begun to recognise this resource as an important one for nature-based tourism development.

However, the primary objective of any national park director in India is to manage the ecosystem to provide for the widest possible range of flora and fauna, including the protection of endangered species. Rarely is he or she involved in tourism development; however, the directors are ultimately responsible for the regulation and limitation of tourists in the national parks. In principle, he or she is governed by the Wildlife (Protection) Act (1972). This was intended as the first comprehensive legislation for the control and management of wild animals and their habitats; however, it is mostly concerned with the prosecution and punishment of offences against wildlife rather than the active promotion of wildlife tourism. The promotion of so-called 'wildlife tourism' is left in the hands of the national Ministry of Tourism and Culture and the various regional state ministries of tourism. Hence, the Ministry of Environment and Forests is concerned that the national park areas will not be harvested for commercial exploitation and they question a consumer-orientated approach. However, this is unrealistic as the parks are already open to unplanned commercial pressures (Figure 5.1).

The different priorities and agendas of the two ministries at governmental level have led to conflict. The conflicts between the Ministry of Environment and Forests and the Ministry of Tourism in India are also complicated by the role of

*Figure 5.1* Unplanned nature-based tourism development, Karnataka.

a number of sub-apparatuses and para-apparatuses that constitute the wider state apparatus in India (see Chapter 2). Indeed, the national parks are managed by the elite bureaucrats of the Indian Forest Service (IFS) and the Ministry of Tourism has little power and influence in this domain. Alongside the key authoritative role of the IFS bureaucrats there are a number of other key groups involved in the current debates surrounding forestry: wildlife conservation NGOs, private sector timber industrialists and rural social activists NGOs. Each of these 'interest groups' is putting forward its own theory of resource use both in the present and for the future (Gadgil and Guha, 1995).

The first group, the wildlife conservationists, exert an influence on forest policy out of all proportion to their relatively small number. Their interests are 'submerged in the philosophy of biocentricism which validates strong action on behalf of the rights of non-human nature' (Gadgil and Guha, 1995: 151). Wildlife conservationists also share a similar educational and cultural background to members of the IFS. The timber industrialists, on the other hand, are the polar opposite of the wildlife conservationists: 'The industrial view of nature is simply instrumental. The forest is a source of raw material for processing factories, and the pursuit of profit dictates a pragmatic and flexible attitude towards its management' (Gadgil and Guha, 1995: 151). However, 'in response to the environmentalist challenge of the past two decades . . . . Some industrialists have been quick to develop their own general theory of resource use' (Gadgil and Guha, 1995: 151). This has been couched in terms of a philosophy of 'national progress' and 'national prosperity'. Rural social activists, on the other hand, are equally polemical in their stand against current forest exploitation in favour of local community forest or joint forest management schemes (Sunder, 2000). To Gadgil and Guha's discussion one can add another interest group, namely that of the private tourism developer (Hannam, 2004a). These entrepreneurs represent another, altogether more ambivalent, interest group. On the one hand they may tend to side with the rural social activists, as they claim that tourism development will lead to jobs and a general improvement in livelihoods. On the other hand they believe that they have the interests of wildlife conservation in mind when they are promoting travel to their private resorts adjacent to the national parks. They are generally critical of the industrialists whom they perceive as threatening their resource base. Conversely, they are criticised by the government's IFS and the other competing groups for their lack of understanding and knowledge of the impact that their own activities have on the same resource base. The 'scientific' experts of the IFS have ultimate control of the forests and have a tendency to adjudicate on the claims of the other interest groups. They often incorporate the expert discourses of the wildlife conservationists to help legitimise their own concerns. The language of expertise is particularly important as the scientific claim to disinterested truth appeals to the ambitions of a number of different interest groups at the same time. In practice, members of the IFS have, thus, been 'able to act on the basis of narrow self-interest, tenaciously clinging to control over all forest areas and the discretionary power that goes with this control' (Gadgil and Guha, 1995: 153). The 'mutual antagonism' of this network of interest groups surrounding forest management in India has led to a situation of stalemate and has prevented any meaningful change in the way that forests are managed in relation to local interests and has thus led to further problems in terms of tourism.

Hence, the development of nature-based tourism in India is widely seen by the IFS as a threat as it is seen as potentially bolstering the power of both private entrepreneurs and state para-apparatuses such as NGOs. The IFS is also at pains to retain its jurisdiction over the environment in India and does not take kindly to interference from officials from the Ministry of Tourism and Culture. In some cases it has closed down nature-based tourism projects funded by the Ministry of Tourism and Culture on grounds of cleanliness. By and large, the current IFS has, as its primary objective, the protection of forests and the environment; tourism is seen at best as a necessary evil to be suffered that deflects attention away from protection efforts. The IFS thus remains the powerful agent of environmental management and tourism development limitation in rural India. Nevertheless, nature-based tourism continues not only to exist in India's network of national parks and wildlife sanctuaries, but also to grow in line with the rise in domestic and international tourism numbers (see Chapters 6 and 7). This situation has led to increasing conflicts between indigenous communities living in and around the national parks as well as between the other interest groups discussed above.

The rights of indigenous tribal populations and their relationships with national park authorities and, indeed, tourism development are also highly problematic in India (Goodwin, 2002; Kothari *et al.*, 1995; Sekhar, 1998; Maikhuri *et al.*, 2001; Young *et al.*, 2001). The situation is especially acute as fuel wood from forests is acknowledged by the Ministry of Environment and Forests as the predominant source of energy in rural areas. As we have already noted, in India the conservationist impulse has largely taken over from any interest in developing tourism. Some eco-development projects have been conceived and implemented around the national parks; however, the main objective is to conserve biodiversity by reducing 'the biotic pressure by alleviating the hardship faced by villagers' but not necessarily through tourism development. Many of these schemes are, in fact, designed to compensate and rehabilitate villagers who have been 'induced' to relocate outside of national park boundaries. Although tourism is only tolerated at present, there are many opportunities for the coordinated development of nature-based tourism in India. As Goodwin (2000: 256) has pointed out:

> The way in which national parks are managed for tourism will have significant effects on the opportunities for local communities to diversify their livelihoods and improve their standards of living by engaging with the tourists who come to their area. Park managers can encourage tourists to visit other natural and cultural heritage attractions in the area, to purchase sustainably produced art and craft products, and to enjoy complementary locally owned products, extending length of stay and increasing visitor spend in the local economy. Tourism is not the only development opportunity that may be available to local communities living adjacent to national parks, but

that opportunity ought to be evaluated alongside others and to be pursued wherever possible.

Indeed, the author of the management plan for Nagarahole National Park has emphasised that: 'A satisfied tourist is the best carrier of the message of conservation' (Appayya, 2001: 185).

Nevertheless, if we look at tourism in India's national parks we can see that tourist behaviour in the national parks is highly regulated, with strict rules on movement (see also Chapter 2). India's national parks attempt to implement codes of conduct for tourists (both domestic and international) by using very basic explanation boards concerning the 'dos' and 'don'ts' of behaviour. Such codes of conduct are essentially a passive or soft visitor management tool aimed at reducing visitor impacts and modifying visitor behaviour (Mason, 2002). However, visitor codes in India's national parks have been seen to be largely ineffective because of a lack of enforcement as well as poor implementation and targeting (Reeve and Edwards, 2002). Furthermore, Mason (2002) has suggested that such codes of conduct assume that the visitor is guilty until proven innocent and largely ignore the role of visitor experience. He argues that, rather than simple codes of conduct, the development of visitor experiences through holistic interpretation strategies should not only lead to better informed and better behaved visitors but also lessen the adverse impacts that codes of conduct are often aimed at. In a similar vein Eagles and McCool (2002) have argued that understanding visitor characteristics, motivations and expectations is the key to effective management. For example, the current management plan for the Nagarahole National Park in Karnataka state recognises this and notes that the park has inadequate interpretive media for environmental education such as appropriate signage, an interpretation centre, publicity material and trained guides.

In general, national parks in India, like other tourism attractions, operate a dual pricing structure in terms of entrance fees, with overseas visitors paying approximately ten times the rate of domestic tourists (with additional charges for compulsory guides, as well as vehicles, elephant rides and cameras). In this context, Goodwin (2000: 255) has argued that:

Dual-pricing systems facilitate access for nationals while enabling a revenue maximisation strategy to be applied to international tourists. The setting of park entrance fees is one aspect of the total management of national parks; it is a complex issue involving a number of trade offs. While increasing revenues from tourists visiting national parks is not a zero-sum game, a strategy of revenue maximisation may lead to increased conflict with local communities, if their opportunities to earn from tourism are reduced by changes in the visitor profile caused by changes in park entrance fees.

The dual pricing system with additional charges that operates in Nagarahole, as in all other national parks in India, is widely resented by foreign tourists to the extent that they frequently shorten their visits (see also Chapters 4 and 6). This fact has been acknowledged by the forest department and is seen as a good thing as it regulates the numbers of visitors. On the other hand, it has led to neither revenue maximisation nor the development of new earning opportunities from tourism for local communities. Many national parks in India also offer various 'tourism experiences' in order to 'manage' the tourists' expectations. This frequently involves the 'staging' of encounters with wild animals for both domestic and international visitors. However, problems arise because of the different aspirations of international and domestic visitors (see Box 5.1). The former frequently portray neo-colonial attitudes and expect preferential treatment. This stems partly from the differential fees that they are charged but also because of their widely different motivations for visiting the parks. Domestic tourists tend to visit in family groups and at present engage with India's national parks as sites of leisure and entertainment, whereas international tourists engage with India's national parks primarily as sites of tourism and for contemplation of nature.

However, all visitors seem to expect to see a wide range of wildlife in a relatively short space of time. Yet the performance of animals in the wild for tourists is not reliable – nature does not often perform at the right time. Indeed, the notion of the timing of 'wild' events is an important distinction here – if nature is manipulated spatially or temporally then the site loses its authenticity and value for the 'ecotourist' – he or she might as well go to the zoo – thus the tourist is left at the mercy of nature for a performance, unless the tourist has sufficient time and money to spend a lengthy period looking for specific species. Thus, the surveillance of particular species as a tourist experience has become important in the Indian context, as elsewhere, in order to verify that there is a chance of an encounter. If the chance falls too low tourists may indeed go elsewhere (Hannam, 2004a).

Outside of the national parks of India, the predominant way in which both domestic and international tourists engage with nature is through India's vast network of zoos. Indeed, and somewhat ironically, some international tourists have felt that their experiences of India's national parks have become 'zoo-like' because of the traffic congestion in the parks and the staging of experiences. Again, as with the national parks discussed above, India's zoos are also places that have led to various conflicts over interpretation, as we discuss below.

## Tourism and zoos in India

As we have discussed above, India is widely known to have a unique fauna, including mega-vertebrates such as tigers, elephants and rhinoceroses, and many of these animals can be seen in the wild in the numerous national parks around the country. Indeed, for many international tourists this is the primary means by which they engage with India's natural world. However, for much of the domestic population, living in the expanding Indian metropolises, the primary means by which they engage with the Indian natural world is through the zoos that were set up by the British colonial administration in the nineteenth century. There are

---

**Box 5.1 The Rajiv Gandhi (Nagarahole) National Park**

The Rajiv Gandhi (Nagarahole) National Park is located 95 km from Mysore and 90 km from Madikeri, whilst the nearest airport is at Banagalore (235 km away). In terms of its history, the park itself was first established in 1955 by the former Coorg State Government when they declared a 285 sq km area as the Nagarahole Wildlife Sanctuary, named after the River Nagarahole that flows through the park (*Nagara* – snake, *hole* – river). In 1975 the sanctuary was upgraded to a national park and extended. In 1986 this park, along with the adjoining Bandipur National Park and the Wynad Wildlife Sanctuary, Kerala and the Mudumalai Wildlife Sanctuary, Tamil Nadu, were included in the wider Nilgiri Biosphere Reserve. In 1992, to mark the first anniversary of Rajiv Gandhi, the former Prime Minister of India's death, the park was re-named in his honour. The current size of the park is estimated at 643 sq km (Manjrekar, 2000). In 2000 the park was included in the Ministry of Environment and Forest's Project Tiger scheme. Significantly, the park is currently part of a wider eco-development project of the Ministry of Environment and Forests. The main aim of this project is the conservation of biodiversity and involves targeted interventions in 'village development'. The project is supported financially by the Global Environment Facility (GEF) and the International Development Agency (IDA) funds of the World Bank (1997–98 to 2002–3) to a value of US$68 million. However, the raising of these plantations was stopped in 1979. In terms of tourism, access to the park itself is generally from buses and taxis that ply from the major cities of Bangalore and Mysore to Nagarahole itself. The park currently has two tourism zones, situated around Nagarahole and Sunkadakatte respectively. The former caters mainly to day visitors and has minimal accommodation, while the latter caters to the tourists visiting Jungle Lodges and Resorts (an upmarket project set up by the Karanataka State Government), based at Karapur at the southern end of the park. Annually 35,000 to 40,000 tourists visit the national park (25,000 to Sunkadakatte, 10,000 to Nagarahole), approximately 8000 of whom are from abroad.

(Appaya, 2001: 51)

---

thus many zoos in the urban centres of India, which serve as a key recreational experience for domestic inhabitants. Most of these are generally in a relatively poor state of repair and have been frequently criticised by international visitors and Western media. In her recent historical review of zoos in India, Sally Walker (2001) has distinguished three phases of zoo development in India. She has argued that the first phase began with the maharajas or princes and continued into the colonial state. The second phase, post-independence, was supported by the central and state governments of India, and she then argues that a third phase is just beginning in the twenty-first century with a review of zoos in India. Walker (2001) discusses how princely menageries kept for intellectual curiosity, scientific enquiry and hunting predate public zoos, but these were nevertheless often open to guests. Indeed, she cites Edwards, who argued that 'zoologists of the early nineteenth century drew much inspiration from collections in India and elsewhere in Asia, rather than the other way round' (Walker, 2001: 252). As Mullan and Marvin (1987) argue, although the formal, traditional zoo was later imposed on India during the British colonial period, the British clearly drew upon these earlier collections. Walker (2001: 254) discusses how a certain Colonel Flower inspected India's zoos in 1913 and commented how 'an enormous number of animals are herded together in no particular order' and that it was a 'very, very sad sight to see the large number of crippled or aged animals which were kept there alive instead of being put out of their misery' in a case of 'misdirected kindness'.

Walker (2001) further noted that many of the zoos in the major Indian cities of Calcutta (Kolkata), Madras (Chennai), Bombay (Mumbai), Trivandrum and elsewhere under colonialism were open to both Indian and European visitors and were particularly enjoyed by children, but the management of India's zoos during this period remained solely under the control of the British administration who were mainly interested in the loss of game for sport rather than any real conservation effort. Initially after independence in 1947, the Indian Board for Wildlife instituted a special 'zoo wing' to review the welfare and scientific utility of India's zoos. In 1972 the Indian Wildlife (Protection) Act, meanwhile, made provisions for the management and development of new zoos in India. As Walker (2001: 286) noted in this regard:

> [m]any [of these zoos] were founded, no doubt, simply to keep up with the next city or state; zoos had become a token of prestige . . . it is safe to say many of the zoos were set up for the wrong reasons. Time [has] proved this to be the case when they deteriorated, lacking the continued personal interest of the individual who set them up, and without a mechanism to ensure their proper upkeep.

By 1975 there was great concern about the quality of zoos in India and an expert committee reviewed them recommending a central coordinating body to monitor and administer them, but it was not until the late 1980s that the Central Zoo Authority (CZA) was finally established and enshrined in the 1991 Zoo Act of the Indian parliament. The main functions of the CZA were to specify minimum standards for zoos in India, to periodically evaluate them and to coordinate training, research and educational programmes. However, it also was given the power to 'de-recognise' zoos after inspection. This is fraught with difficulties, though, not just because of the bureaucracy that this entails but also because of Hindu religious and social customs that largely disavow the taking of life even if it is to end suffering (see also Chapter 7). Thus, in the contemporary period, Walker (2001: 251) notes that '[i]n India, a country with a history of extreme kindness to animals on the one hand and inordinate cruelty on the other, there were until recently well in excess of 300 collections of wild animals in captivity registered with the Central Zoo Authority'. The CZA (2009) currently states that:

> Since its inception in 1992, the Authority has evaluated 347 zoos, out of which 164 have been recognised and 183 refused recognition. Out of 183 zoos refused recognition, 92 have been closed down and their animals relocated suitably. Cases of the remaining 91 derecognized zoos are currently under review. The Authority's role is more of a facilitator than a regulator. It, therefore, provides technical and financial assistance to such zoos which have the potential to attain the desired standard in animal management. Only such captive facilities which have neither the managerial skills nor the requisite resources are asked to close down.

Walker (2001) goes on to argue that many of the zoos in India are problematic in terms of overcrowding, both of animals and of people, and argues for the need for zoos in India to be privatised so that they might be run better, with less bureaucracy and with greater investment. Moreover, she further argues that India's zoos have so far failed to develop a single scientific breeding programme and have also failed to live up to their educational and conservational potential. She concludes that '[p]erhaps Indian zoos should just concentrate on educating their public to protect its remaining habitat' (Walker, 2001: 290). We can see that these problems are still current by looking at the case of Mumbai's zoo (Box 5.2).

Zoos have been rather under-recognised as a potential tourism resource in India (Hannam, 2011). In his seminal paper on tourism and zoos, Peter Mason (2000) argued that zoos are a form of living museum (see also Chapter 4). He

---

**Box 5.2 The Veermata Jijabai Bhosale Udyan Zoo**

The city zoo, which has been receiving flak since the death of a five-year-old hippopotamus in April, is all set to adorn a new look by the year 2012. After receiving green signal from the Mumbai Heritage Committee for the Rs 433 crore modernisation plan last week, Byculla Zoo Authorities, is now awaiting approval from the Standing Committee of the Brihanmumbai Municipal Corporation (BMC). . . . However, animal rights organisation are strongly opposing the modernisation plan. The animal rights organisation have claimed that currently the enclosures are not designed to fulfil the biological needs of the animals as it does not resemble the natural habitat of the animal. 'We don't want animals to be showcased for entertainment of people. Zoo's are expected to provide visitors an opportunity to learn about nature and wildlife but in this case, city Zoo Authorities lack the expertise and inadequate infrastructures. The very idea behind Zoos is inherently flawed in the first place,' said animal activist Fiza Shah.

(DNA India, 2009)

went on to discuss that zoos are important from a tourism perspective in terms of both amusement and education. However, the most important functions of zoos are arguably their educational aspect and to make animals available for viewing as well as to generate excitement for visitors who would otherwise never see such animals in real life, particularly charismatic and rare mega-vertebrates, except perhaps in films (Bostock, 1993; Shackley, 1996; Mason, 2000; Ryan and Saward, 2004). Although visitor motivations for visiting zoos may be varied and complex it has been generally recognised that zoos may provide important cognitive and affective educational experiences for visitors (Churchman, 1985; Hunter-Jones and Hayward, 1998). Sophie Turley (2001: 8), meanwhile, has emphasised the importance of zoos as social recreational experiences, particularly for children who 'both facilitate and, in their absence, inhibit zoo visiting'. Furthermore, she notes that previous research has argued that many zoo visitors are only mildly interested in the animals per se, with the actual visit having more importance as a family social event.

Bostock (1993: 109), meanwhile, has noted that contemporary 'zoo architecture often seems to have been a rather misguided pursuit, aimed at pleasing human taste instead of serving the animals' own interests'. He went on to further argue that the 'best' enclosures are 'naturalistic' ones that provide the 'illusion' that the animals seen are 'in the wild' but such 'furnishings' may be for the benefit of the human visitors as much as they are for the animals themselves (Bostock, 1993: 113). Furthermore, he concluded that there are 'obviously' grades of keeping animals in 'prison-like' captivity, with the unintentional and intentional unpleasantness of such captivity being morally wrong (Bostock, 1993: 122). As Mason (2000: 336) notes:

> If zoos are viewed as unacceptable visitor attractions by some people, then they may fail to provide appropriate educational messages, particularly in terms of conservation. The conditions in which animals are kept may even deter visitors and there is currently some evidence to support this.

However, Ryan and Saward (2004: 249) point out that 'there is an argument that market forces may lead to the betterment of zoo design to the advantage of animal welfare and conservation programmes, and to the financial advantage of zoos by being more attractive to visitors'. Catibog-Sinha (2008), meanwhile, argues that zoos in developing countries still operate under substandard conditions and many are managed mainly for amusement and entertainment. The aesthetics and purpose of zoo design in developing countries, of course, are fraught with difficulties because of funding (Figure 5.2).

## Conclusions

This chapter has critically examined the various contemporary conflicts involved in the use and management of nature-based tourism in India. We have taken a political ecology perspective in analysing the relationships between tourism

*Figure 5.2* Mumbai Zoo.

and the environment in India. First, we have conceptualised nature within the Indian context by drawing upon tourism and leisure narratives from the colonial period in terms of hunting and conservation. Then we have discussed the conflicts involved in the management of India's national parks as tourism resources. Finally, we examined the similar conflicts involved in the management of India's zoos. The next chapter moves on from our consideration of various contested tourism resources in India to consider the voices of international tourists in the Indian context.

# 6  International travel and tourism to India

## Introduction

This chapter examines international tourism flows into India. It begins by critically examining international tourism flows into India from the eighteenth and nineteenth centuries from a post-colonial perspective and it draws upon much of the travel-orientated literature to do this. In so doing it also outlines the cultural encounters between the West and India that continue to influence the dominant perception of the country in the West. The chapter then discusses how, from being a predominantly international backpacker tourist destination in the twentieth century, India now attracts a much broader range of international tourists as a gradually enhanced infrastructure has made India a more attractive destination in the twenty-first century. Finally, this chapter also examines the development of new markets such as medical tourism and health tourism that have been at the forefront of contemporary tourism developments in India.

Back in the early 1990s it was acknowledged that the growth of international tourism to India faced an image problem due in part to poor accommodation and transport and sanitary conditions as well as tiresome bureaucracy and political uncertainty (Chaudhary, 1996). Historically, there was a relatively low priority and 'lack of urgency' afforded to international tourism development by the government of India (Raguraman, 1998). In the twenty-first century, however, this is changing as the numbers of international tourist arrivals to India have witnessed growth rates well above average world figures. Moreover, the Indian government is beginning to recognise the importance of diversifying its tourism products. In terms of this diversification, as we have seen in previous chapters, religious and heritage tourism have been particularly highlighted (Joseph and Kavoori, 2001).

Currently just over half of India's foreign tourists come from Western Europe and North America and the vast majority are non-package 'backpacker' tourists or independent travellers who stay for at least one month. Tourism has a marked seasonality in India, with October to March being the predominant season. India has largely failed to develop any 'package' tourism industry except at places such as the former Portuguese colony of Goa (Wilson, 1997). Perhaps the most significant contemporary change has been the shift towards organised mass tourism to destinations such as Kerala. Along with the growing Indian middle class and the consequent socio-cultural and economic change, India increasingly displays a more typically Western supply of hotels, restaurants and even transport. These developments have been pushed forward by both the Indian media and the Indian government in order to attract a more affluent range of travellers (see also Chapter 2). Nevertheless, India has always appealed to middle-class foreign tourists, particularly, it has been argued, because of various orientalist representations, which we discuss below.

## Conceptualising international tourism to India

The dominant paradigm in tourism research would suggest that tourism is largely about an escape from home and from the mundane aspects of everyday life. Within this conceptual framework it makes sense to assume that tourists often seek encounters with what we might term exotic environments, cultures and practices. Although we do not, in this book, see the exotic in direct opposition to the familiar, we do need to explore the way in which many international tourists view destinations such as India as being more or less exotic. India has been represented and stereotyped as exotic, as the 'Other', by both the infrastructures of tourism and the cultural industries that support it (including travel writing, place marketing, film and computer gaming). We will therefore introduce concepts from post-colonial theory to demonstrate how discourses of the 'Other' reflect dominant power relations in tourism. As Hall and Tucker (2004: 2) note in this context, tourism 'both reinforces and is embedded in postcolonial relationships'. Historically, this has involved the frequent portrayal of India as either a place of paradise or a place of extreme poverty and potential danger, or, indeed, as being both at the same time. There is no denying that many international tourists are drawn to visit India by its sheer exoticism, the extent to which it is perceived to be unlike everyday ordinary life in the West. Such exoticism is widely communicated in the mass media by tourism marketers and place branders through depictions of spectacular landscapes, the picturesque and elements of 'local' culture such as so-called 'colourful' host populations. Nevertheless, there is also a long history to this process of 'Othering'.

The literary theorist Edward Said was the first to critically examine these processes of exoticisation in his seminal text *Orientalism* (1978). His text demonstrated that the social construction of a 'mystic orient' as a distinctive place served primarily to emphasise the 'flexible, positional superiority' of the West (Said, 1978: 7). He drew implicitly and explicitly on the philosopher Foucault's proposition that power and knowledge are intimately related through a gaze on the 'Other'. He developed a critique of the binary oppositions that pervade the stereotyping of places, one side of which is seen as superior to the other. Hence, for Said (1978), the social construction of the Orient exists only as a counterpoint to the Occident (the West). The Orient is socially constructed as a place where those in the West can contemplate their fantasies and desires outside of their own boundaries of normality. Thus, the fabricated 'mystic orient' is frequently seen as a relatively timeless, unchanging and anachronistic place. Hence, in such a timeless 'Other' we find contrasting and conflicting representations of the Orient (East) that stress luxury and excess or cruelty and intrigue or, indeed, both simultaneously. There is no doubt about the seductive power of the symbolic systems at work in the construction of such orientalism in both tourism and inter-related forms of popular culture more widely (Shurmer-Smith and Hannam, 1994). Importantly, Said (1978) even recognises that many orientalists (and tourists) frequently 'love' the countries that they visit as privileged onlookers; however, they cannot escape being bound up in the ensuing power relations.

In terms of examples, we do not need to look very hard in India to find evidence to fit Said's arguments. They are all around us in the mass media – films, advertisements, literature and even computer games. These representations insinuate themselves into everyday taste in clothes, food, interior design, perfume and even politics. And, crucially, they also inform much of travel writing and, more importantly, people's choices of where to go in terms of tourism. The current UK Thomas Cook website, for example, describes how:

> Goa has a more European feel. The invasion of the Portuguese in 1510 brought with it a Mediterranean influence that can still be seen today. Like Kerala, the beaches and scenery are description-defyingly beautiful. Goa has everything the holidaymaker could want, with a healthy sprinkling of Indian exoticism and mystery.

However, the narratives of colonial exploration and discovery also have a strong echo in many of the narratives of contemporary tourism, which implore us to explore and discover. Interest in exotic landscapes and people can be traced back to the 'heroic' era of exploration in the eighteenth and nineteenth centuries. For example, Thomas Cook first published his *Cook's Indian Tours* in 1889 and this guidebook argued that 'India presents wide fields of observations for all classes, but more especially for the geologist, botanist, zoologist, archaeologist, and the artist' (cited in Epelde, 2004: 119). This emphasis on nature-based tourism links back to our discussion in Chapter 5. However, Cook was also instrumental in developing the first outbound 'tours' of England for Indian princes (see also Chapter 8). Around 5,000 Indians were transported to England in the nineteenth century but many found themselves the object of the Western tourist gaze as 'exhibits' at the Colonial and Indian Exhibition, held in London in 1886 (Epelde, 2004).

Moreover, the era of 'heroic' exploration in the nineteenth century has perhaps now been supplanted by an era of 'heroic' volunteer tourism and student educational visits (see Wearing, 2001). Such visits can, of course, be seen as a legacy of the earlier era of geographical exploration and fascination with the exotic, and in many cases continue to be about the promotion of 'development'. We recognise, however, that a great deal of contemporary tourism is also packaged and sold on the basis of an engagement with and experience of exotic places, as well as the opportunity to explore and discover new people, cultures and landscapes. Whichever type of tourism we examine, we cannot think about the exotic without realising that there are always complicated, and historically based, power relations involved in the attaching of stereotypes to both people and places.

Although Edward Said's (1978) critique of orientalist practices was mostly concerned with the power relations that underlay the representation of places, other critics have criticised Said's work as too simplistic and have put forward alternative theories of the post-colonial condition. Furthermore, the cultural theorist Homi Bhabha (1994) criticises Said's conception of orientalism as too homogeneous. Instead, Bhabha (1994) sees orientalism as fundamentally ambivalent in its character; it is both a discipline of learning and discovery and a fantasy based around certain myths. Bhabha thus distinguishes between 'manifest' orientalism – the conscious body of scientific knowledge – and a 'latent' orientalism – an unconscious desire (Young, 1995). Moreover, he argues that Said (1978) allows little room for the resistance to colonial power and desire except from his own exterior position; the very ambivalence within the colonial project itself allows for a certain amount of resistance to take place. Bhabha (1994) re-examines colonial stereotypes in this context and finds that it is not that the stereotype is simply crude in relation to the complexity of the people, but rather it is itself a complex, ambivalent, contradictory, anxious and assertive mode of representation.

Hence, drawing on Bhabha (1994), we can begin to understand how indigenous hosts in non-Western countries come to resent in part the cultural impact of visitors who bring with them such stereotypes (see Hollinshead, 1998, 2004). Such cultural stereotypes and impacts of tourism are of course frequently contested (even violently). In the contemporary world, because of globalisation processes, new forms of orientalism and place stereotyping are present in tourism discourses as both people and places become more mobile. Thus, in terms of contemporary tourism, the attitude towards India is still ambivalent, combining the older patronage evident in discourses of orientalism with a newer engagement with economic and technological power. Moreover, as India becomes more 'known' as a tourist destination, many international tourists seek more 'dangerous' and 'extreme' destinations, venturing up into the north-east states of India in search of more remote and exotic experiences.

However, conversely, as outbound tourism from India to the West develops, many Indian tourists may now socially construct the West as a site of decadence and nostalgia. The exotic, of course, is not always located a long way away from home, and can be found in some domestic tourism encounters, which become even part of destination branding in terms of ethnic tourism (McKercher and Du Cros, 2002; Diekmann and Maulet, 2009). For example, eating Indian cuisine has long been a favourite British leisure pastime, with chicken tikka masala arguably one of the favourite dishes. Many international tourists' first 'taste' of India is through its food and by visiting Indian ethnic enclaves such as Southall in London (see Chapter 8).

## Western travellers' accounts of India

Western travellers have been visiting and writing about India since the fifteenth century when the Russian horse dealer Afanasy Nikitin visited India (Fisher, 2007). Many of these early Western travellers to India were motivated by commercial imperatives and for them India was a much wealthier country than the European kingdoms from which they ventured (Fisher, 2007). Moreover, such early travel accounts of Mughal India 'for all their flaws and errors and occasional fictions and tall stories, and despite the prejudices and sometimes outright bigotry of their authors, do nevertheless tend to provide sharper and certainly livelier pictures of the reality of Mughal India' (Dalrymple, 2007: vi–vii). Furthermore,

> [a]lthough the early European travellers were sometimes surprised or even disgusted by what they found in India, their reactions seem to be far more the result of helpless vulnerability before this great Islamic power . . . rather than the snide hauteur of some of the Victorians.
>
> (Dalrymple, 2007: ix–x)

Travel writing in the colonial period meanwhile may be regarded in the context above as one of the 'apparatuses of the empire' (Mohanty, 2003: xiii). Mary Louise Pratt (1992) in her seminal book *Imperial Eyes* clearly demonstrates the complex and diverse connections between travel writers' accounts and the histories of imperialism and colonialism. Many of these colonial travel accounts focused on the attractiveness of native Indian women, frequently using racist and pejorative terminology. S. Menon (2003: 103), for example, cites the example of James Forbes's comment that 'the Hindoo women when young are delicate and beautiful, as far as we can reconcile the idea of beauty with the olive complexion'. Indian men on the other hand were frequently represented as being 'effeminate' in character in these Western travel accounts.

Sara Mills (1991), meanwhile, has demonstrated that many of the colonial travel accounts of non-Western societies were written by women (see Box 6.1). And, again, rather ironically, many of these female English travel writers tended to resort to the feminisation of Indian men with all the colonial associations of inferiority therein (Mahajan, 1996; Dalrymple, 2003; S. Menon, 2003; Blunt, 2005). Often neglected, however, are the travel accounts of Indian travellers in their own country during the colonial period. Mohanty (2003: xv–xvi) notes in this context that:

> [i]n the Oriya author Sashibhusan Ray's Dakhinatya Bhramana, (Travel to the South), 1897, for example, we see precisely such a trend. There is much local colour here, aside from a discovery of new lands and regions. But there is also the self's encounter with the mighty power of the British Empire.

Contemporary travel writing, meanwhile, depicts the exotic through the lens of the individual traveller or backpacker who has to overcome (and suffer) a series

---

**Box 6.1  Emma Roberts on travelling in India**

In a dak journey, the traveller must apply to the postmaster of the place of his residence to furnish him with relays of bearers to a given point. . . . An oblong chest will convey the truest idea which can be given of this conveyance; the walls are of double canvas, painted and varnished on outside, and lined within with chintz or silk, it is furnished on either side with sliding wooden doors. . . .

The stages vary from ten to fourteen miles and a change of bearers is often effected in the midst of a wide plain. The relay, which is generally in waiting for some time, kindle a fire, group themselves around it, and beguile the interval with smoking or sleeping. . . .

In the hot season, persons who brave the heat of the day in a palanquin, venture at the risk of their lives: they should always take care to be houses by twelve o'clock.

(Roberts, 1935: 203–209, cited in P. Nayar, 2009: 34)

---

of rites of passage in order to move from being a tourist to being a fully accomplished traveller in an exotic world (see Hannam and Ateljevic, 2008; Hannam and Diekmann, 2010). Such 'suffering' is of course constructed as an 'authentic' experience in the glorification of being a traveller consuming the exotic, in contrast to the tourist who consumes the familiar. Michael Palin (1989), for example, has done much to resurrect the white male traveller who consumes the exotic in a light-hearted way, but, rather than being part of the colonial enterprise, Palin's travel becomes an initiation ritual (see Box 6.2).

In the same vein, William Sutcliffe (1997) and Sarah MacDonald (2003) in their respective accounts *Are You Experienced?* and *Holy Cow!* have also both described in an irreverent style their discovery of the cultural variety of India, but also their encounters with discovering themselves and how travellers tend to search for the company of other travellers rather than to really get involved with their Indian hosts. The former BBC correspondent Mark Tully's (1991) and William Dalrymple's (1998) travel accounts, meanwhile, are more critical and reflective of both the historical and contemporary cultural imperialism that has taken place in India arising from processes of globalisation and, of course, tourism itself. Both are perhaps a little guilty though of a Western romanticisation of India's early pre-colonial past.

## Culture shock and contemporary backpacker tourism to India

Nevertheless, the perception of India in the West often leads to passionate positive and negative feelings. There is a common story narrated by many Indian taxi drivers and local workers around airports that some 20 per cent of all international

**Box 6.2  Michael Palin on India**

We pull up at Dadar Station at two o'clock, our minibus driver sliding in beneath a sign reading 'Parking For Four Bullock Carts Only'.

Train travel in India is not restful, and the shredding of the nerves begins as soon as you enter the station. The Indians seem to revel in the arguments and misarrangements and hustle and heat and chaos. Though my name is clearly spelled out on the computer-printed list of passengers, posted on the platform: 'Michael Palin . . . male . . . 45 . . . 194/64', it appears that there are two other people called Michael Palin in 194/64, and one of them is a woman.

Part of the problem is that Indian Railways is the largest civilian employer in the world, and for every single problem you have there are about eight people all with different ideas of how to solve it. A hapless man called Mr Nitti has been detailed to accompany us and look after all our needs. He is nowhere to be seen.

We leave on time at 2.30. Our journey across 1251 kilometres of India will take 27 hours and we shall make 30 stops. The implacable couple called Michael Palin sit resolutely surrounded by BBC equipment, quite unmoved by the entreaties of the recently located Mr Nitti. I sit in the corridor with the window open, glad to feel a breeze on my face and glad to be circumnavigating again. I could well do with a cool Kingfisher beer but the only bars on this train are across the windows.

(http://www.palinstravels.co.uk/book-1327)

tourists take the first plane out again when they come out of the airport. Although there is no scientific evidence for this particular narrative, some studies have evidenced a return home earlier than planned because of various aspects of cultural confusion as well as health problems (Hottola, 2004). In comparison with many other destinations, the announcement that one is leaving for India always creates rather strong reactions, such as 'How can you? There is so much poverty', 'I could never go there', 'You must be well prepared otherwise you won't be able to stand it'. The other extreme reaction is envy, jealousy, compassion and the wish to go there too. These reactions show that the contemporary travel narrative on India still draws upon the much older discourses of orientalism that we have discussed above. Moreover, these reactions are very much based on emotional factors influenced by the previously mentioned travel writers and the media and rarely on an empirical understanding. These reactions can be linked to what the anthropologist Oberg (1960) called 'culture shock'.

According to Irwin (2007: 1) culture shock is 'anxiety and emotional disturbance experienced by people when they travel or move to a new social and cultural setting when two sets of realities and conceptualizations meet'. It is about losing familiar representations and well-known values and being confronted with very different behavioural patterns. Oberg (1960) divided culture shock into four different stages: honeymoon, crisis, recovery and adjustment. However, not each traveller goes through all stages according to Oberg and Irwin. In their view, tourists hardly ever cope with the last three stages for they return home before the honeymoon ends (Irwin, 2007). Although the stages may be too categorical as they do not take into account individual perceptions and experiences of culture shock, they can to a large extent reflect experiences described by some international travellers (Mumford, 1998). From the perspective of Irwin, the honeymoon stage refers to upmarket tourists staying in upmarket hotels and only staying for a short period in the host country. The second stage is often encountered in travel narratives, when travellers have to cope with the real conditions of life in the country. Indeed it should be added that some international visitors do intentionally search for these 'real life experiences' (see Chapter 3). This phenomenon can be observed particularly with backpackers staying in India for longer periods. Some French authors have also focused on conceptualising mental disorder while visiting India, calling it the 'India syndrome', comparable to the Stendhal syndrome describing the impossibility of coping with the environment in the host country (Magherini, 1992). Régis Airault (2002), a psychiatrist who worked for many years in the French embassy in Mumbai, has described the culture shock phenomenon in relation to India and argues that many individuals travelling to India do have some psychological issues before coming and therefore choose this particular country in order to find themselves and help themselves to get out of their troubles. Conversely, he also describes 'healthy' Western travellers coming to India and finding themselves confronted by culture shock and then suffering from depression or similar psychological problems.

Hottola (1999, 2002, 2004) and Graburn (2001), however, have been critical of the culture shock thesis and write more about a process of 'cultural confusion'. In his thesis based on in-depth ethnographic research in India, Hottola (2002: 83) noted that the 'profusion of sexual advances towards Western women travellers was found to be the most important source of intercultural confusion and conflict between Western visitors and their hosts in India'. Varma (2004: 3) meanwhile has described the cultural confusion from the perspective of a host thus:

> Those who do (come to India) mostly come to discover an ancient culture and find it in amazing monuments strewn carelessly across the land. They have read about spiritual India, and see the soaring pinnacles of the temples of South India and in the devotees taking a dip in the Ganga in Varanasi. The diversity of food and dress devours the reels in their cameras. They buy handicrafts at cheap prices as proof of the incredible exotica they had been promised. They find modern India in the English speaking Indian and the high-rise buildings in the metropolises. The tout who cheats them is proof of the essential corruption of underdeveloped economies. The filth and poverty is nauseating but is hazily attributed to the timeless other-worldliness of spiritual India.

This account perhaps summarises the contemporary 'backpacker' experience of India. As we noted above at the beginning of this chapter, India has, since the 1960s, been a key destination for independent travellers and so-called backpackers. Rory MacLean (2006: 204–205) has written of how:

> The sixties travellers arrived in India with a feeling of homecoming, as much to themselves as to the country. After the long and overland trail, the road broadened out into the subcontinent's hundred cities and thousand choices. The Intrepids, carried forward by Ginsberg's first article on India in City Lights Review and Kerouac's vision of a Rucksack Revolution, fanned out, slowed down, looked to find a place of their own. Some headed south to Rajasthan, with its pink medieval city of Jaipur rising out of a yellow desert. Others went north to Kashmir's lakes. Most travelled straight to Delhi, usually asleep on third-class carriage luggage racks. There the inner quest usually began at the Crown, a rose-scented, bug-infested hotel with shacks on the roof. Almost everyone turned up, tuned in and dropped out.

MacLean (2006) emphasises how the backpacker to India of the 1960s and 1970s was often on a Western-style pilgrimage in search of a guru to follow as had been popularised by the Beatles following their visit to India. Such pilgrimages have continued in the contemporary period with so-called *ashram* tourism. Sharpley and Sundaram (2005) have considered the recent motivations and experiences of Western tourists visiting the Sri Aurobindo Ashram and the nearby utopian township of Auroville in Pondicherry. They identify two principal groups of visitors, namely permanent tourists who have immersed themselves indefinitely in spiritual India, and temporary visitors with a variety of spiritual and non-spiritual motives.

Nevertheless, backpackers – spiritually minded or not – have continued to be the main international tourism market for India. Indeed, backpacking is increasingly part and parcel of the wider mainstream tourism industry in the twenty-first century and has arguably become normalised and institutionalised through increased mobilities (Hannam and Diekmann, 2010). Kant (2009), the former Ministry of Tourism secretary, however, has dismissed backpacker tourism rather too quickly in favour of older, more affluent tourists, arguing wrongly that 'backpackers and budget travellers pay for their entire holiday in the country of origin. They tend to spend less money once they are here, quite unlike affluent travellers'. Debates in the academic literature have variously categorised them as either 'more environmentally friendly' (Scheyvens, 2002) or the 'perpetrator of global spread' (Wheeler, 1991: 92). Some researchers further argue that the contact between backpackers and local people is more intensive than that between other tourists and local people (Aramberri, 1991), whereas others argue that backpackers have a tendency to primarily socialise within their own enclaves and ignore local people (Maoz, 2002). Indeed, in his novel, Sutcliffe (1997) tells the story of Dave who goes backpacking because everyone else is. Dave's enthusiasm for meeting a fellow Briton whilst travelling in India is tried when he receives a biting analysis of backpacker travel from him:

University of Life ... got to the Third World and survived. No revision, interest or sensitivity required ... it's not hippies on a spiritual mission who come
here anymore, just morons on a poverty-tourism adventure holiday .... Your
kind of travel is all about low horizons dressed up as open-mindedness. You
have no interest in India, ... and treat Indians with a mixture of contempt and
suspicion which is reminiscent of the Victorian colonials.

(Sutcliffe, 1997: 138)

Mowforth and Munt (1998: 135), meanwhile, suggest that, rather than being
somehow ethically concerned tourists, backpackers can be included in the category
of self-centred tourists that they call 'ego-tourists' or 'curriculum-vitae builders'.
However, 'while self-gratification and indulgence may be the primary motivation
for one category of backpackers, others may be driven by a genuine interest in
learning about other people and environments, and many may fall somewhere
between these extremes' (Scheyvens, 2002: 150). The literature is clearly divided
as to whether backpackers exhibit socially ethical behaviour, or whether they are
just 'ego-tourists' in search of 'self-gratification'.

Another common criticism of backpackers is that, in ensuring that their funds
will last for the duration of their travels, they become obsessively focused on
budgets and bargain-hunting (Bradt, 1995; Goodwin, 1999). According to Riley
(1988) 'status among travellers is closely tied to living cheaply and obtaining
the best bargains which serve as indicators that one is an experienced traveller'.
Backpackers have been described as exploiting their powerful market position, as
they use guidebooks, sometimes seriously dated editions, to establish prices and
then try to secure accommodation at a lower price (Goodwin, 1999). Research in
Australasia, however, has challenged this, finding that because of longer trip duration, backpackers actually spend more than other tourist categories (Scheyvens,
2002). Through purchasing locally produced goods and services, backpackers
also contribute significantly to local economic development (Riley, 1988; Wilson,
1997; Hampton, 1998). Indeed, Wilson (1997) argues that, in Goa, backpackers
are welcomed because their needs are easily serviced, resulting in an industry
characterised by 'wide local ownership of resources and the broad distribution
of benefits throughout the local community'. Furthermore, Hampton's (1998)
research has argued that backpacker tourism can become one way of increasing
local participation within a sustainable and ethical development strategy.

Nevertheless, it is widely accepted within the literature that often backpackers
pave the way for mass tourism (Cohen, 1972, 1973; Butler, 1990; Wheeler, 1991).
Furthermore, one of the key developments in backpacker tourism in recent years
has been in terms of the notion of the 'flashpacker' (Jarvis and Peel, 2010; Hannam
and Diekmann, 2010). The so-called flashpacker has emerged as a new and key
constituent of contemporary travel and exemplifies the changing demographics
in Western societies where older age at marriage, older age of having children,
increased affluence and new technological developments, alongside increased
holiday and leisure time, have all come together (see also Chapter 8). The flashpacker has thus been variously defined as the older twenty- to thirty-something

backpacker, who travels with an expensive backpack or a trolley-type case, stays in a variety of accommodation depending on location, has greater disposable income, visits more 'off the beaten track' locations, carries a laptop, or at least a 'flashdrive' and a mobile phone, but who engages with the mainstream backpacker culture. Or more simply defined on Travelblogs.com (2009) as backpacking 'with style' or even backpacking with 'bucks and toys'. Indeed, with the growth in global mobilities we increasingly see these so-called international flashpackers visiting India with very different expectations from the 'traditional' backpacker.

Recent research by Scott Cohen (2010) also reminds us of a different phenomena, the lifestyle tourist, who, like the earlier 'drifter', still spends the majority of his or her life indefinitely 'on the road' engaged in the backpacker culture – which remains a feature of international tourism to India. For both the flashbacker and the lifestyle traveller, however, it has to be recognised that new technologies have transformed the ways in which they travel and engage with their home place and their social ties (see Chapter 8). However, it can also be noted that the backpacker tourism market in India is still dominated by many younger and less affluent tourists who spend most of their time in what have become mainstream and even institutionalised backpacker enclaves. Furthermore, although ostensibly engaging with the exotic by visiting India, many Western tourists fall back on the familiar and retreat to a meta-spatial bubble or enclave whilst they are there (Edensor, 2001; Hottola, 2005; see Figure 6.1). Based upon his ethnographic research in India, Hottola (2005: 5–6) elaborates five categories of meta-spaces where independent travellers segregate themselves:

*Figure 6.1* Backpacker enclave, New Delhi.

1   Private spaces reserved for travellers such as rooms in hotels and guest-houses or even washrooms which may provide a protective shield against the eyes of the Others.
2   Semi-private spaces of restricted access such as shared areas in private houses with rooms to rent and guesthouses and hotels where their restaurants and gardens are open only for paying customers or invited guests. Segregation from public space is often enforced by gatekeepers, walls and fences. Occasionally, Indian travellers may share accommodation with backpackers but many Indian guesthouses do not accept (the more demanding) indigenous customers. The company of fellow travellers serves as a buffer against culture confusion.
3   Public spaces of restricted access. Most of the touristic spots where entrance fees are collected belong to this category. In India such places are, in practice, closed for the common public who cannot afford to pay the fees. The same applies to other places where separation is based on difference in economic standing, such as airline offices, expensive restaurants, first class train carriages and many museums.
4   Spaces of temporary Western domination. This category includes the beaches of Kovalam in Kerala or Mamallapuram in Tamil Nadu, and other major backpacker gatherings such as Pushkar Cattle Fair in Rajasthan or Hampi in Karnataka, where the sheer number of Westerners constitutes them as a temporal majority.
5   Wilderness areas where human population is low and intercultural contacts can, therefore, be reduced easily to a comfortable level for Western tourists, if necessary.

The phenomenon of backpacker meta-spaces or enclaves in India has been further researched, in particular by Darya Maoz (2006, 2007). She describes how, following military service, young Israelis travel for prolonged periods to India and have subsequently established Israeli backpacker enclaves in New Delhi, Goa and Manali and favour specific travel routes as they move around India:

> Participant observation showed that most young Israeli backpackers tend to settle in certain districts in India, setting up Israeli enclaves in specific and well-known places. In their enclaves the backpackers continue, to a large extent, their Israeli life. Most of the food is what the backpackers consider Israeli, the menus are written partly in Hebrew, and so are the signs hanging in the streets. The backpackers read Hebrew books and Israeli newspapers, listen to Israeli music, surf the internet in Hebrew, read and write e-mails in Hebrew and speak only Hebrew, even with the Indians.
>
> (Maoz and Bekerman, 2010: 429)

In other work Maoz (2008) has further discussed the experiences of middle-aged Israeli women who have visited India as independent travellers. Most of the women travellers interviewed by Maoz experienced a 'mid-life crisis', and the backpacking journey to India was perceived as a chance for transformation, overcoming fears and difficulties and finding a new meaning to life.

Beyond the backpacker experience of India, many international visitors have recently come to India for medical and health reasons, and we turn to this aspect next.

## Medical and health tourism in India

Recent international tourism arrivals to India have also been fuelled by the rise in medical and health tourism. The idea of health tourism can be traced back to the eighteenth and nineteenth centuries when spas and healthy seaside or mountain resorts developed to provide rest and cures for people with diseases such as tuberculosis. At this time, travel to treat illnesses usually consisted of a long-term trip, with people spending weeks or months at a destination. Smith and Puczko (2009: 6) go on to argue that the concept of health tourism, however, can mean very 'different things in different countries and cultures'. They note that:

> Chan's (2007) research in Malaysia showed that local people associated health and wellness mainly with personal wellbeing and lifestyle, stress release for working people in urban areas and a new form of leisure/tourism activities for foreign tourists. This includes spa and body treatments for personal wellbeing (stress release) and beauty/cosmetic surgery. In Central and Eastern Europe, the term health is closely related to physical and medical healing. . . . Many Western Europeans are familiar with the concept of historic, thermal spa tourism as well as thalassotherapy (cures based on sea elements), especially on the Atlantic coast. In Southern Europe there is an emphasis on seaside wellness, where sunshine, sea air and thalassotherapies are used to enhance wellbeing. In addition, the pace of life is relaxed and siestas are common, and the Mediterranean diet is considered to be one of the healthiest in the world. . . . In Scandinavia, there is a large emphasis on outdoor recreation such as Nordic walking, cross-country skiing, and lake swimming, even in winter.
>
> (Smith and Puczko, 2009: 6)

Nowadays health tourism has a broader meaning not necessarily linked to an illness but as a remedy for routine fatigue and stress with many tourists combining a 'recovery' and 'well-being' trip with conventional sight seeing. Former health-care destinations have been redeveloped to satisfy a new clientele that is no longer as subsidised by public health services. Studies of health tourism have tended to emphasise a contrast between Asian countries, where more spiritual and mindful activities such as yoga, massage and meditation are the norm, and Western countries, where cosmetics, pampering, physical healing and medical treatments are more common. However, because of globalisation processes, these contrasts are increasingly becoming blurred. In recent years numerous hotels in India have been built or refurbished to offer both the spa treatments that are commonly available in many Western health resorts and Indian treatments. Moreover, the classical Indian treatments such as Ayurveda (see Box 6.3 and Figure 6.2), yoga and meditation have also been increasingly exported to the West and can now be found at many Western health resorts. However, in this context, Hannam (2009: 343) has noted that:

> Kerala was the first State in India to sell health tourism abroad by promoting Ayurveda. However, it has recently been recognised by the Government of India that 'the oversell of Ayurveda has resulted in the mushrooming of unlicensed and ill-equipped healing centres which often have untrained and unqualified personnel. There has also been a growth of shady spas and massage parlours in the garb of Ayurvedic treatment'.

Many Western tourists also now visit India for medical treatments (George, 2009). Such medical tourism is a relatively new phenomenon in many developing countries, which provide medical treatments at lower prices for Western visitors.

---

### Box 6.3  Defining Ayurveda

Ayurveda has been described by various practitioners as:

- 'a complete and integrated life science'.
- 'the science of life and the art of living'.
- 'a holistic , spiritual and philosophical system of medication that covers all the principals of Allopathy, Homeopathy and Naturopathy'.

From the Sanskrit, Ayurveda is derived from *ayu* (life) and *veda* (knowledge) and is some two thousand years old. Ayurveda views the world as having an intrinsic order and any illness is a departure from that order. According to Ayurvedic philosophy we all possess three *doshas*, humours or elements, namely: *vatha* (wind or air), *pitha* (fire) and *kapha* (water/earth). Any disease is diagnosed as an imbalance of these in the human body. Treatments, therefore seek to restore the balance of these three elements by either *panchakarma* (internal purification), or diet and massage. Contemporary Ayurveda in Kerala is largely focused on forms of massage, which is claimed to be particularly beneficial for those suffering chronic ailments such as arthritis and rheumatism. However more austere treatments are available including induced vomiting, herbal applications through the nose, medicated enema, and (under medical supervision) surgical drainage of the blood. Having an ayurvedic massage in Kerala is primarily relaxing and widely available at most hotels but treatments need to be sustained over two weeks or more for any further benefits (Hannam, 2009).

*Figure 6.2* Ayurveda clinic, Kerala.

The rise in medical tourism is due, in part, to the weakened and expensive health-care systems that exist in the United Kingdom and the United States, and in part to the development of an online brokerage system that attempts to match potential patients with particular hospitals in particular destinations (Connell, 2006). The promotion and marketing of medical tourism also has to convince potential clients from developed countries of the availability of modern technologies, a high-quality service and overseas staff training (Connell, 2006). Moreover, as Bookman and Bookman (2007: 29) note, 'visitor expenditure outside their hotels can range from half to nearly double of the in-hotel expenditure'. Hence, the importance of tourism destination marketing for medical tourism development should not be underestimated. According to Kant (2009) there is now a debate as to whether insurance companies should cover the costs of medical tourism.

In contrast to health tourism, medical tourism deals only with short-term interventions, with the most common medical procedures being heart surgeries, knee and hip replacements and cosmetic surgeries (Bies and Zacharia, 2007). In India specific destinations have become specialised in specific treatments. For instance, heart surgery patients are recommended to go to New Delhi, whereas eye surgery patients are recommended to go to Chennai (Hazarika, 2009). India has also become a centre for medical tourism because of its reputation for having highly skilled surgeons and because of its additional advantage of having the support of a mix of allopathic and alternative systems of treatment (Hazarika, 2009). Medical tourism is also one of the new tourism products to be actively promoted by the Ministry of Tourism in India (see Box 6.4). In its 2008–9 annual report,

## Box 6.4  Government promotion of medical tourism in India

India is a perfect destination for medical tourism that combines health treatment with visits to some of the most alluring and awe-inspiring places of the world. A growing number of tourists are flocking in large numbers because of the superlative medical care, equipments and facilities that India offers.

India excels in providing quality and cheap health care services to overseas tourists. The field has such lucrative potential that it can become a $2.3 billion business by 2012, states a study by Confederation of Indian Industry (CII). In 2004, some 150,000 foreigners visited India for treatment, and the numbers have been rising by 15 per cent each year.

India is in the process of becoming the 'Global Health Destination' owing to the following advantages:

- The cost of medical services in India is almost 30% lower to that in Western countries and the cheapest in South-east Asia.
- Language is a major comfort factor that invites so many foreign tourists to visit India for medical and health tourism. India has a large populace of good English speaking doctors, guides and medical staff. This makes it easier for foreigners to relate well to Indian doctors.
- Indian hospitals excel in cardiology and cardiothoracic surgery, joint replacements, transplants, cosmetic treatments, dental care, Orthopaedic surgery and more.
- The medical services in India include full body pathology, comprehensive physical and gynecological examinations, audiometry, spirometry, Chest X-ray, 12 lead ECG, 2D echo Colour Doppler, gold standard DXA bone densitometry, body fat analysis, coronary risk markers, cancer risk markers, high strength MRI etc.
- All medical treatments and investigations are done using the latest, technologically advanced diagnostic equipments.
- Indian doctors have got an expertise in performing successful cardiac surgeries, bone marrow transplants, liver transplants, orthopaedic surgeries and other medical treatments.
- The cost of Infertility treatments in India is almost 1/4th of that in developed nations. The availability of modern assisted reproductive techniques, such as IVF, and a full range of Assisted Reproductive Technology (ART) services have made India the first choice for infertility treatments.

(http://india.gov.in/overseas/visit_india/medical_india.php)

the Ministry of Tourism extended the Market Development Assistance (MDA) scheme to include medical tourism. Thus, the Ministry now provides financial assistance to Medical Tourism Service Providers (MTSP), that is, representatives of hospitals accredited by the US-backed Joint Commission International or the Indian-backed National Accreditation Board of Hospitals and Medical Tourism Facilitators (Ministry of Tourism, 2009a: 29). At the same time, the Ministry has produced a brochure on medical tourism and asked state tourism departments to promote medical tourism through clear and precise information on the best hospitals, prices and packages available. Moreover, for the purpose of supporting medical tourism, a new category of 'medical visa' has recently been introduced by the Ministry of Home Affairs. A study by McKinsey projects that medical tourism in India has the potential to generate almost US$2 billion by 2012 (cited in Kant, 2009: 166). However, the ethics of medical tourism need to be noted in this context. It needs to be remembered that the vast majority of the ordinary Indian population still do not have access to primary health care. Hence, in order to be successful, medical tourism needs to have a positive impact on the local communities as well as on the Western tourist.

## Conclusions

This chapter has examined various international tourism flows into India. It began by conceptualising the notion of orientalism and how this then pervades much travel writing about India. The chapter then discussed how India developed into a twentieth-century backpacker tourism destination, and subsequently how India now attracts a much broader range of international tourists. Finally, this chapter has also examined the development of health and medical tourism in India. The next chapter moves our discussion on to consider aspects of domestic travel and tourism in India.

# 7    Domestic travel and tourism in India

## Introduction

This chapter explores the development of domestic tourism in India, which has been widely viewed as being on the rise in recent years. It draws upon current debates on changing Indian social structures to critically analyse the key trends in domestic tourism in India, from honeymoons to weekend breaks. Because of the recent economic growth in India, India's middle class represents a growing consumer group that is increasingly integrating and blending more western-ised lifestyles with aspects of domestic culture. The domestic tourism sector is also benefiting from newly renovated infrastructures and accommodation. Nevertheless, we argue that domestic tourism in India has been, and still remains, largely centred around issues of pilgrimage, and hence in this chapter we also explore the significance of pilgrimage in the Indian context by synthesising a range of research.

According to Ahuja (1999: 19) domestic tourism was defined for the first time in India in 1977. In this definition a domestic tourist is a person who travels within the country to a place other than his usual place of residence and stays at hotels or in *dharamshalas*, *sarais*, *musafirkhanas*, *agarshlas*, etc. for any of the purposes of (a) pleasure, (b) pilgrimage, religious and social functions, (c) business, confer-ences and meetings and (d) study and health. Rao and Suresh (2001: 208), mean-while, similarly define a domestic tourist in India as a person of Indian nationality who travels within India and stays in 'Indian-style accommodation for pleasure, pilgrimage, religious and social functions, business conference, study and health'. In tourism research, primary attention has generally been given to international tourism and intercultural exchange between hosts and guests. Yet, in terms of numbers, domestic tourism including travel for pilgrimage, visiting friends and relatives (VFR), etc. represents an important market. Indeed, S. Singh (2009b) states that, in comparison with Western tourism research, Asian domestic tourism needs an Indian perspective. In this context, a distinction can be made within the domestic tourism sector in India. Gladstone (2005) separates what he calls the domestic formal sector from the domestic informal sector. The first refers to the new middle classes with a more westernised leisure lifestyle, whereas the second refers to pilgrims and other travellers. Whereas middle-class domestic tourists can be approached from the classical Western academic point of view, this is more difficult when it comes to informal domestic 'travellers'. Singh (2009b) points out that, in the Western construct, tourism is generally perceived as an institutionalised or formalised provisioning, whereas the Eastern construct, related to pilgrims and VFR, adheres more to local norms of social conduct. She further argues that:

> quite unlike international/modern tourism that relies heavily on global systems, where researchers refer to super- and supra-structures as being crucial to its rituals, Asian domestic tourism seems to have evolved and sustained itself in the absence of heavy investments and commercialisation as being vital to its rituals.
>
> (Singh, 2009b: 3)

Hence, in what follows we are keen to avoid a purely Western view of India's domestic tourism and attempt to conceptualise this phenomena in terms of mass tourism developments as well as highlighting the continuing centrality of pilgrimage in India.

## Conceptualising domestic tourism in India

Rao and Suresh (2001) have noted that domestic tourism in India has historically had three key dimensions:

1 Traditional – pilgrimage to and fairs and festivals at various Hindu, Buddhist, Muslim, Sikh and Parsi shrines. As we shall see, pilgrimage is still a significant part of the domestic tourism experience in India.
2 Historical – pleasure and leisure activities of the nobility. This refers to the various mobilities of the Mughal period, which have been replaced in the contemporary period with the very different mobilities of the hyper-mobile Indian elite.
3 Colonial – hill stations and beach tourism were developed by the British in the late nineteenth century and also drew a domestic audience. Again, this has its contemporary corollary as domestic Indian tourists have been instrumental in furthering the mass tourism development in the hills, mountains and beaches of India.

More recently, with the advent of a more westernised lifestyle, a fourth dimension has been added, namely themed cultural, heritage and nature-based tourism, such as reconstructions of, for instance, Rajasthani villages. Gladstone (2005: 130) describes his experience thus:

> On the night we went there, the park was crowded with Indian families who all seemed to be having a very good time. Children and their parents would take rides on camels and elephants; scream as the Ferris wheel operator spun

them up and down on the manually operated ride; view traditional Rajasthani (or what was staged as traditional Rajasthani) puppet shows, magic shows, and dances; and eat a meal sitting down on an earthen floor in a building designed to evoke images of what is supposed to be a typical Rajasthani village dwelling.

As we shall see, the potential of domestic tourism has grown substantially during the last few years as a result of an increase in income levels and the emergence of a dynamic urban middle class. Rao and Suresh (2001: 205) also recognise that the Indian railways, in providing special trains and concessions, played 'a significant role in enhancing the number of domestic tourists'. This pattern has now changed with the massive growth of the domestic airline industry in India in the contemporary period.

Although the Ministry of Tourism (2009b: 58) concedes that 'there are no precise estimates of total domestic tourist traffic in the country', state governments reported that the number of domestic tourists during 2007 was estimated to be 527 million, showing a growth of 13.9 per cent compared with 2006. The last survey of domestic tourism in India was undertaken in 2002 by the Ministry of Tourism in conjunction with the National Council for Applied Economic Research (NCAER). This survey reported domestic tourism as being primarily for social motivations (60 per cent) such as VFR or attending births, marriages or funerals, followed by religious motivations (14 per cent), business travel (8 per cent) and holidays (6 per cent) (Ministry of Tourism, 2003).

Rao and Suresh (2001) acknowledge that it was not until the late 1990s, as the economic liberalisation policies began to kick in with the concomitant rise in India's middle classes, often with double incomes, that the Indian government and, indeed, the Indian tourism market began to recognise the potential of the Indian domestic market as a relatively low-cost investment opportunity. However, Rao and Suresh (2001: 207–208) also note that 'standards and costs to the domestic tourist remain beyond the means of most urban dwellers and are far from satisfactory' and largely 'below their expectations'. Government policy on domestic tourism is still regarded as 'ambivalent' at best and we need to acknowledge that, in terms of the domestic market, travel takes place against an economic background of widening disparities between the rich and the poor in India.

Although, at independence, domestic tourism was seen as part of the agenda for national integration and nation building (see also Chapter 2), up until the twentieth century this was largely given lip service with the majority of resources concentrated on the growth in numbers of international visitors, primarily because of the need to earn foreign currency and because of support from international bodies such as the World Trade Organization (WTO). As a result, many local fairs and festivals that have previously drawn domestic tourists have been largely appropriated by the state and subsequently commodified as international tourism products beyond the means of the domestic tourist, despite dual pricing policies. Rao and Suresh (2001: 205) note that the dual pricing policy has divided 'different sections of the travel trade, with the tour operators supporting the "fair trade" stand of the international customer and the accommodation units fighting for higher occupancy by lowering rupee tariffs for the domestic business'.

However, although in the 1980s government support for domestic tourism was largely passive, the Youth Hostel movement was actively supported, along with some adventure and camping activities, particularly to underdeveloped areas of India, so that the urban 'youth' could learn about rural India. Moreover, 'it was noted that pilgrim flows formed an important part of domestic tourism and infrastructure and facilities needed upgrading at pilgrim centres' (Rao and Suresh, 2001: 204). The Ministry of Tourism in India recognises, year on year, that these pilgrimage centres have exceeded their carrying capacities and that the management of numbers attending particular holy festivals needs to be increased: '[p]ilgrims have been staggered, held back, often faced the rods of security forces and shrines have been shut down to allow the rest of the staff to perform rituals, and yet the numbers keep increasing every year' (Rao and Suresh, 2001: 204).

Alongside government initiatives, the recent impact that the media – particularly television programming and newspapers – have had on the domestic audience in India in the promotion of travel for travel's sake also needs to be recognised (Gladstone, 2005; Rao and Suresh, 2001). Joining forces with the Indian, largely state-controlled media, the Indian government has, for example, spearheaded the promotion of domestic tourism into the north-eastern states such as Assam, Arunchal Pradesh, Tripura, Meghalaya and Nagaland – areas for which international tourists find it difficult to secure a 'special permit' to visit, but which the Indian government is keen to integrate further into the Indian polity because of frequently violent secessionist movements. Of course, the latter are often keen to vent their frustrations by targeting the domestic tourist, which has frequently thwarted these government-led promotional tourism development efforts. Conversely, both the state and tour operators in other destinations, such as Kerala and Goa, that continue to rely heavily on international tourists as part of their economic growth plans have specifically ignored and even attempted to deter relatively lower-spending domestic tourists from visiting.

Still, a significant proportion of domestic tourists in India remain pilgrims. Hence, we discuss this in the following section before going on to examine the development of middle-class package tours in India.

## Pilgrimage and domestic tourism in India

A key aspect of India's domestic tourism is encapsulated in the notion of pilgrimage. India is a secular country but home to many religions, each with a different history of pilgrimage. In this section we discuss the different ways in which pilgrimages are utilised by members of different religious faiths in India: Hindu, Sikh, Buddhist and Muslim. Of course, it is as well to remember that pilgrimage in India, as elsewhere, '[a]part from the devotional aspect . . . involves sightseeing, travelling . . . and buying local memorabilia, almost everything a tourist does' (Gupta, 1999: 91).

Indeed, Turner and Turner (1978) in their classic analysis demonstrated many

connections between tourism and pilgrimage, despite different underlying motivations. Importantly, they argue that any form of pilgrimage involves aspects of
*communitas* – commonly defined as an acute point of community spirit. In their
book Turner and Turner (1978) distinguish between three types of *communitas*
involved in pilgrimage. First, existential *communitas* – a more or less spontaneous
spiritual inter-relatedness by a religiously informed community in which pilgrims
voluntarily celebrate common humanity. Second, normative *communitas*, which
represents the ways in which religious specialists in particular attempt to regulate
pilgrims and their shrines in an institutionalised process. Third, ideological *communitas* can be defined as the remembered tributes of the *communitas* experience
at a particular site or sites of pilgrimage. This model of pilgrimage has been highly
influential in studies of pilgrimage and tourism (see E. Cohen, 1992; MacCannell,
1992).

However, the concept of *communitas* put forward by Turner and Turner (1978)
has come in for some criticism. Sallnow (1981: 179) has argued, somewhat
pertinently in the Indian context discussed below, that there is a 'complex interplay between the social relations of pilgrimage and those of secular activities'.
Moreover, John Eade (2000) has argued that the notion of pilgrimage needs to
be situated within the very contested political and cultural processes that actually shape pilgrimage. Further, Eade (2000) argues that we need to deconstruct
the category of pilgrimage into historically and culturally specific behaviours –
something we attempt to do in an introductory way below in the Indian context
as there is no uniform notion of pilgrimage, rather an interwoven, and frequently
contested, embodied and performative triad of person, place and text. Thus, the
following discussion of pilgrimage also needs to be considered within the wider
context of tourist mobilities and the de-territorialisation and de-traditionalisation
of leisure practices (Rojek and Urry, 1997; Sheller and Urry, 2004; see also
Chapter 8). Clearly, in this chapter we could also discuss aspects of Buddhist,
Jain, Christian, Jewish or Zoroastrian pilgrimage in India, but we will concentrate
on the three major religions of Islam, Sikhism and Hinduism to illustrate some of
the main issues and conflicts involved.

### Hindu pilgrimage

Hinduism is widely regarded as the world's oldest surviving religion, the majority
religion in India and the third largest worldwide numerically, after Christianity
and Islam. Hinduism is a polytheistic faith that reveres several gods and goddesses who are deemed to have control over the creation of the world, life and
nature. It is also an extremely tolerant religion in that it recognises all religions as
having the same goal. Unlike other religions, however, it has no founding prophet
or individual authority. It does, however, have a series of sacred texts, written
largely in the form of epic stories, by which individual Hindus may learn how to
achieve piety (R. A. Singh, 2006). In an important paper Rana Singh has charted
the notion of pilgrimage for Hindus in India. He argues that 'Travel for pilgrimage purposes is an important part of Hindu doctrine and millions of adherents

travel throughout India and from abroad each year to participate in enormous festivals, pilgrimage circuits and ritual cleansings' (Singh, 2006: 221). According to the Hindu scripture the *Mahabharata*, pilgrimage places are auspicious for Hindus because of either their earth or water, or because they were made holy by visits by various sages or wise men. By travelling to these sites and performing sacred rituals there, Hindus may transform or cleanse themselves of their mortal sins. Pilgrimage for Hindus, then, is a spiritual quest of the highest order and highly valued as a rite of passage. To quote Singh (2006: 222) once more, 'Hindu pilgrimage involves three stages: initiation (from the time one decides to take the journey to the beginning of the journey), liminality (the voyage itself and experiences involved), and re-aggregation (the homecoming)'. Singh goes on to note a set of key principles associated with Hindu pilgrimage (see Box 7.1).

In her detailed ethnographic study of Hindu pilgrimage in the state of Maharashtra, Feldhaus (2003) emphasises the importance of water and indeed rivers for Hindu pilgrimage. She notes three particular kinds of river pilgrimages. First, the practice of circumambulating a river; second, the pilgrimage rituals in which people carry representations of village gods or goddesses to a river to be bathed; and, third, pilgrimage rituals in which people fetch water from a river to bathe a representation of a village god or goddess.

Sagar Singh (2004: 56), meanwhile, has argued that significantly in Hindu pilgrimages:

> [t]he caste (*jati*) structure is important in understanding the dynamics of pilgrimage and change. Traditional institutionalised pilgrimage was meant to be secular in a sense: ritual purity and pollution of castes was de-emphasised and people of all castes (excluding the untouchables) were allowed to undertake the journey and see the deity.

---

### Box 7.1  Key principles of Hindu pilgrimages

- Part of religious duty implies being free from other worldly duties.
- One should seek the support of deity to fulfil the journey.
- One should seek religious companionship while travelling.
- There should be a desire to enhance fellowship in the sect they are associated with.
- Pilgrims should seek to understand the sacred symbols and knowledge of shrines.
- One should try to encounter new areas.
- Difficult and arduous journeys are a form of penance.
- Pilgrimage is an opportunity to improve overall well-being, harmony and happiness.

(After Singh 2006)

Although this could be disputed (see Feldhaus, 2003), it is also evident that the notion of Hindu pilgrimage in the contemporary era has been both commodified and, indeed, realised by state intervention, as we discuss further below.

In terms of Hindu pilgrimage, perhaps one site stands out as being of particular importance in terms of our discussion of domestic tourism and that is the sacred festival called Kumbha Mela – the largest pilgrimage gathering in the world. This is a riverside festival held four times every twelve years that rotates between the city of Allahabad located at the confluence of the two rivers Ganges and Yamuna, the town Nasik on the Godavari river, the town Ujjain on the Shipra river, and the village of Haridwar on the Ganges (Bhardwaj, 1973; Dubey, 2001; Feldhaus, 2003). As R. A. Singh (2006: 228) notes: 'Bathing in these rivers during the Kumbha Mela is considered an endeavour of great merit, cleansing both body and spirit. The Allahabad and Haridvar [sic] festivals are routinely attended by millions of pilgrims'. During this festival the Kumbha Mela is actively performed through ritual bathing, chanting, singing, giving to the poor and debating the various Hindu scriptures (see also Box 7.1). Bathing in the Ganges, in particular, is viewed as a symbolic process of spiritual cleansing. With the ever-increasing numbers of both domestic and international tourists visiting these festivals, sustainability issues also come to the fore.

In this context, Shinde (2007) has recently examined the environmental impact of domestic Hindu pilgrimage to the Hindu holy town of Tirupati in southern India. He concludes that:

> the environment in Tirumala-Tirupati is subjected to two interrelated pressures: direct pressures related to increasing visitor flows and indirect pressures of rapid urbanisation induced by economic opportunities from regular visitation. These pressures affect the environment in three interrelated ways: (1) stress on basic services (water supply, sewerage, and solid waste), (2) pollution (mainly air pollution) and (3) degradation of natural resources (forests, groundwater).
>
> (Shinde, 2007: 356)

From a more political perspective, meanwhile, Singh (2006) goes on to discuss how the revival of traditional Hinduism in the 1950s led to the popularisation of pilgrimages and, in turn, a further assertion of Hindu identity, leading to conflicts with other religions in India. Such conflicts are typified by the destruction of the Babri Mosque at Ayodhya in December 1992 by Hindu nationalist groups wishing to build a Hindu temple on this site, which is reputed to be the birthplace of the Hindu god Lord Rama and the site of an eleventh-century Hindu shrine (Mandal, 2003). As a consequence of this, large civil disturbances ensued in India in the 1990s and resurfaced again in 2002. Indeed, Corbridge and Simpson (2006) have charted the use of Hindu pilgrimage for political purposes by militant Hindus since the 1980s. In particular, the militant Hindu nationalist political parties have organised a series of large processions or *yatras* that traverse the country symbolically in an attempt to figuratively map a specifically Hindu geography. Bonney

(2003), meanwhile, notes that there are a very large number of potential sites in India that could be claimed by both Hindus and Muslims as one or the other had previously enjoyed rights of worship at that location. He cites the example of the Mughal Qutb Minar complex in Delhi, built in 1192 on the site of twenty-seven razed Hindu temples where Hindu nationalists have recently tried to hold Hindu rituals and prayers.

### Sikh pilgrimage

Globally the Sikh population is estimated at over 20 million, the vast majority of whom live in the state of Punjab in India, forming some 2 per cent of the total Indian population. However, some 3 million Sikhs live outside India and represent a significant and influential diaspora, particularly in the United Kingdom, the United States and Canada (Hannam, 2004c). As a religion, Sikhism was founded in the fifteenth century by Guru Nanak based upon the concept of the universal equality of all people. His message was developed by a further nine gurus who shaped the Sikh community by providing various scriptures and institutions. The last guru, Guru Gobind Sing, in the seventeenth century, encouraged male Sikhs to adhere to five practices, namely to not cut their hair (to symbolise their spirituality), to carry a small wooden comb (to symbolise their cleanliness), a steel bracelet (to symbolise strong will and self-restraint) and a small sword (to symbolise truth and justice), and to wear knee-length shorts (symbolising moral purity). He also prescribed that Sikhs wear a turban, which at that time had had previously been the reserve of royalty. The Sikh holy book – *Guru Granth Sahib* – passed down from Guru Bodind Singh, is placed in Sikh temples known as *gurdwaras*. Those *gurdwaras* associated with Sikh history have become important places for Sikh pilgrimage. Unlike Hinduism and Islam, Sikhism does not encourage its followers to go on a pilgrimage in search of spiritual purification; rather pilgrimage is seen as an external activity largely devoid of inner devotion, or indeed as a rather futile activity spiritually. Rather, it emphasises the inner spiritual journey that a person must undertake to become a better person and Sikhism discourages 'blind ritualism, image worship and visits to scared rivers and tombs' (Jutla, 2006: 211).

However, despite the emphasis in the Sikh scriptures on the non-necessity of pilgrimage, in actual practice Sikhs do enact pilgrimages, primarily as a historical (heritage) rather than as a spiritual recollection. On Sikh pilgrimage, Jutla (2006: 207) notes that:

> On September 1, 2004, between 3 and 4 millions of Sikh pilgrims from all many corners of the globe visited the Golden Temple at Amritsar. This occasion marked the four hundredth anniversary of the installation of Guru Granth Sahib, the Sikh scripture, at the Golden Temple.

The Sikh Golden Temple is also a sacred site that has seen recent conflict. In June 1984, the then Indian prime minister Indira Gandhi ordered an attack on armed Sikh militants hiding at the Golden Temple. Over 500 people were killed in the ensuing fighting, and Sikhs around the world were outraged at the desecration of their holiest site. Four months after the attack, Indira Gandhi was assassinated by her two Sikh bodyguards, leading to a massacre of thousands of Sikhs in the reprisals that followed (see Box 7.2).

As we shall see with other forms of domestic tourism development, the sustainability of tourism has become a major issue in India as domestic tourism continues to grow. In this context Shinde (2007: 346) discusses the example of the Hemkunt Sahib, a Sikh pilgrimage centre in the Himalayas that

> attracts more than 150,000 pilgrims during a period of four months in a year. During this time, problems such as [the] accumulation of huge amount of non-biodegradable waste (plastic and glass cups, polythene etc.), water pollution (due to inadequate sewerage facilities), deforestation due to harvesting of firewood, and destruction of flora and fauna are reported. . . . Another problem relates to overcrowding, congestion and stampedes which usually get a lot of media attention.

### Islamic pilgrimage

Clearly, the Islamic pilgrimage to Mecca, Saudi Arabia, is the most significant pilgrimage for Muslim people, and a whole industry exists in India to support this, including special airport terminals. We consider this phenomena further in Chapter 8, which considers India's outbound tourism. In this chapter we can note some of the key features of Islamic pilgrimage within India. India was ruled by an Islamic (Mughal) aristocracy from the sixteenth to the mid-nineteenth century and this left an indelible mark on India's religious and historical landscape. Although the detailed history of the Mughal period in India is beyond the scope of this book, we can examine this landscape. Numerous palaces, tombs and forts built by the

---

**Box 7.2  Mark Tully on Operation Blue Star**

Operation Blue Star, the Indian army's clumsy attack on the Sikh Golden Temple at Amritsar in June 1984, shook the foundations of the Indian nation. It deeply wounded the pride of the Sikhs, the most prosperous of India's major communities. It strengthened the cause of those Sikhs campaigning for the setting up of a separate Sikh state – Khalistan – and gave them a martyr – Sant Jarnail Singh Bhindranwale, the fundamentalist preacher who had fortified the Golden temple complex and died defending the shrine. It caused Sikh soldiers to mutiny. It led directly to the assassination of the prime minister, Indira Gandhi, and to the worst communal violence seen since the partition riots of 1947.

(Tully, 1991: 153)

Mughal dynasty stand in the major cities of Delhi, Agra, Jaipur and Hyderabad. In particular, a number of sites stand out, and one of these is, of course, the Taj Mahal (Figure 7.1).

Although these sites may be visited by Muslims undertaking pilgrimages, they are also very much sites that both domestic and international non-Muslim tourists visit in large numbers. Indeed, the Taj has become a symbol of India as much as the Eiffel Tower is a symbol of France or the Statue of Liberty a symbol of the United States, and this fact was articulated by many of the domestic visitors interviewed by Edensor (1998). He noted that many domestic tourists at the Taj performed a different kind of 'gaze' from that of international visitors:

> it is the fame of the Taj that attracts [Indian] people, its renowned beauty and history. Although first identified as a world wonder in the colonial era, the notion has been appropriated by Indians to enchant their sense of national identity and prestige. However, the desire to see the symbolic site is not accompanied by a desire to gaze at or experience the Taj intensely. Instead, a visit to the Taj is typified by a communal witnessing of a national monument with family, friends or fellow-villagers, as well as millions of other Indians.
>
> (Edensor, 1998: 126)

*Figure 7.1* Taj Mahal, Agra.

Edensor (1998) calls this a 'collective gaze' and distinguishes it from the more common, Western 'romantic gaze' that we discussed in Chapter 4. Although the Taj may not be experienced by domestic tourists using a romantic aesthetic, romance itself certainly does feature at the Taj for domestic visitors as the Taj is a popular spot for Indian honeymooners or those couples seeking to reaffirm their marriages. In so doing, the object of gaze for the domestic tourist is also the international tourist, with many domestic tourists asking to be photographed with the tourists from abroad. These domestic tourists also purchase models of the Taj as important souvenirs (Edensor, 1998).

Furthermore, Edensor (1998) also notes the existence of a domestic mediatised gaze at the Taj, as the Taj is frequently the backdrop to Tamil and Hindi films. But there is also another gaze present at the Taj – what Edensor (1998: 96–97) terms a 'reverential gaze' enacted by Muslim visitors that focuses intensely upon the divine and the sacred:

> Although the Taj Mahal is undoubtedly the result of a synthesis of Indian architectural forms, it is stamped by Islam. Most obviously, one of the large buildings flanking the Taj is a mosque which is usually visited by Muslim visitors to the site . . . the peak season for Muslim visitors to the Taj is during the great December pilgrimage to the tomb of a Sufi saint at Ajmer when thousands en route wait in queues hundreds of yards long to gain entrance to the Taj.

Beyond the religious experience of domestic tourism pilgrimages, India has more recently developed a substantial domestic tourism outside of the religious context. We turn to this next.

## India's middle-class domestic tourism

We now recognise that India has in recent years developed a substantial and sophisticated middle-class population, like many other developing countries. As Gladstone (2005: 131) states, 'the increasing buying power of households has combined with advertising and other media images from wealthy countries (e.g. film, magazines, satellite television) to create the basis for a consumer society in countries that are on the whole desperately poor'. Nevertheless, Beteille (2001: 5) has argued that:

> [t]he Indian middle class, like the middle class anywhere in the world, is differentiated in terms of occupation, income and education. But the peculiarity in India is its diversity in terms of language, religion and caste. It is by any reckoning the most polymorphous middle class in the world.

Moreover, he notes that it has 'an ugly face, and its members often appear as callous and self-serving' (Beteille, 2006: 177). Varma (2004), meanwhile, in the introduction to his book *Being Indian*, enforces this view by deconstructing philosophical perceptions of the Indian 'other-worldliness' and highlighting the cultural characteristics of the Indian middle class. Gladstone (2005: 139) further notes that:

> one of the most evident changes is the shift in both official government rhetoric and the attitude of ordinary citizens from a view of India as a land of poverty and scarcity where 'mindless' consumption has no place to a rampant consumerism characterized by its glorification of the market and its indifference to the sufferings of the poor.

Mawdsley (2004: 85), meanwhile, has also noted that:

> [f]or some commentators, one of the defining features of India's middle classes at the turn of the millennium is their appetite for 'global' culture, and their pursuit of 'western' lifestyles, possessions and values (Gupta, 2000; Lakha, 2000). This is, according to these accounts, a transnational class of people who are bound up in the cultural and economic transactions of contemporary globalisation, and who have more in common and closer social relations with parallel classes in South Africa, Australia and the USA than with the parochialised 'have-nots' of their own nation.

Their number is also steadily increasing. In 2005, Gladstone estimated the number of middle-class individuals to be around 180 million, S. Singh (2009b) talks about a third of the total population and Bandyopadhyay (2008) notes about 300 million.

In this context, we have already noted how, in their overview, Rao and Suresh (2001) highlight the role of colonial sites for the consumption of domestic tourism in India. Moreover, Kennedy (1996) has elaborated on the importance of India's hill stations in terms of the medicalisation of leisure for the British colonial elite in India – places where the Indian was largely spatially segregated, 'tolerated' and seen as 'undesirable' except in a mode of strict servitude. In an interesting paper, Jutla (2000) has discussed this phenomenon using the case of the colonial 'summer capital' of India – Shimla (Figure 7.2), located approximately 7,500 feet above sea level in the Himalayas. Jutla (2000: 406) notes that historically

> the hill station was not only a haven from the hot Indian summer but its winter snowfall allowed for recreational activities such as skiing and skating. The British sought to recreate an English townscape in Shimla. The dense and mature pine forests of the hill station generated an enduring imagery. The image of the city was projected to revive memories of England and this is reflected today in the Gothic and Tudor architecture.

Indeed, the various hill stations in India provided the colonial elite with a recreational space away from the heat and dust of the plains (see also Baker, 2009; Gladstone, 2005).

Although developed for domestic tourism after the second five-year plan in the

*Figure 7.2* Shimla, Himachal Pradesh.

1950s, hill stations have met with tremendous success from the 1980s onwards with the growing new middle class (Chand, 1998; see also Chapter 2). Gladstone (2005) emphasises the fact that the hotel sector in Himachal Pradesh is indeed arguably larger than elsewhere in India. This is confirmed by Jutla (2000) high-lighting the contemporary domestic tourism in Shimla, which has become the most popular 'mass tourism' destination in the Himalayas. Himalayan towns and cities such as Shimla and Manali in the Kulu Valley have, since independence, become must-see destinations, particularly for young couples on their honey-moons and celebrating anniversaries. Much of this mass tourism has been fuelled by the use of the Himalayan scenery in Bollywood films (see also Chapter 3). According to Gladstone (2005), other factors that served to develop Manali's popularity with domestic (and, indeed, international) tourists were the completion of road infrastructure as well as advertising. Significantly, Jutla (2000) also notes that because of the large influx of predominantly middle class domestic tourists, the cultural and environmental sustainability of Shimla and other hill stations are now under threat: 'a number of local residents, local officials and tourists show deep concern for the changing image of Simla. Both tourists and residents fear that the city is losing its character' (Jutla, 2000: 407). This is a problem that many of the colonial hill stations seem to be undergoing (see, for example, Joshi and Pant, 1990, on the environmental problems facing Nainital). S. Singh (2005) notes the recent influx of 'environmental pilgrims' into the Himalayas as domestic tourists respond to the growth in niche tourism products such as heritage tourism and nature-based tourism (see also Gupta, 1999; Mawdsley, 2004; S. Singh, 2004; and also Chapters 4 and 5).

In this context, Mawdsley and colleagues have recently examined the growth of nature-based domestic tourism in India. In line with other studies, they have noted that 'domestic visitors are largely overlooked as an analytical category in academic and policy literatures concerning the politics and management of India's protected areas' (Mawdsley *et al.*, 2009: 49). Moreover, they also noted that 'academic neglect of domestic visitors is reproduced in the training and management structures of Indian wildlife conservation' (p. 50). They went on to argue that:

> a far larger proportion of visitors were lower-middle and middle-income family groups enjoying a day out, work mates on a trip, school groups, and even a large group of teacher trainers on a day outing. They travelled in crowded buses, small cars, hired Gypsies and taxis. Our income, ownership and education questions demonstrated that while almost all the visitors would fall within the top half of India's wealth distribution, the vast majority could not be considered among the 0.4% of families designated 'rich' by the NCAER.
>
> (Mawdsley *et al.*, 2009: 52)

These findings can be confirmed by the authors of this book based upon interviews and observations of domestic visitors at a range of national parks and protected areas in India (Hannam, 2004a) as well as by Edensor's (1998) interviews and observations at the Taj Mahal discussed earlier.

The latest tourism product joining the domestic tourism arena has been the launch in 2009 of a democratic tourist train, comparable to the social tourism provision in some Western countries which offers tourism experiences that are highly subsidised by the government and which are organised for the 'average' person (Costa, 2009). In an article in the *Times of India*, Costa highlights the Bharat Darshan, a special train run by the Indian Railway Catering and, Tourism Corporation (IRCTC), as being a major success with domestic tourists. In contrast to the expensive and upmarket trains the Palace on Wheels and the Golden Chariot (see Chapter 4), this 'common man's palace on wheels' offers all-inclusive 'package' tours around India, including the mass tourism 'hot spots', along with pilgrimage destinations. According to Khanna (2009), the tours, primarily aimed at budget domestic tourists, have also drawn tourists from the middle classes. Because of the success of the train – although there are no official statistics – new routes are now being created, running several times a year and covering more and more states in India, with a particular focus on the hinterland (Khanna, 2009; see Box 7.3 and Figure 7.3).

### Box 7.3  Bharat Darshan special tourist train

'Bharat Darshan Special Tourist Train', one of the most affordable all inclusive tour package, covering all the important tourist places in the country.

The Bharat Darshan tour packages costs Rs. 500/– Per Person Per day, which is inclusive of providing comfort of travel by train in IInd Class sleeper coaches, besides it, the cost is inclusive of following:

1. Hall accommodation at places of night stay/morning freshening up.
2. Quality vegetarian meals.
3. Tourist buses for visiting sightseeing spots.
4. Guides/Tour escorts for announcements and information.
5. Security arrangement for each coach.
6. A Railway Staff on train as Train Superintendent.

Currently Bharat Darshan tours commence from South and West zone only. Booking of Bharat Darshan Special Tourist Trains is available online on our website. Booking can also be done through our Tourist Facilitation Center, Zonal Offices and Regional Offices.

(http://www.bharatdarshantrains.co.in)

*Figure 7.3* Travel by Indian railways.

## Conclusions

In this chapter we have reviewed the development of India's domestic tourism industry. India's domestic tourism is of primary importance to the development of the tourist industry in the country. Along with the 'informal' travellers and pilgrims, new 'formal' markets have opened up through the new middle class in the country. According to Ahuja (1999) the development of tourism in the country still basically caters to the demands of domestic tourists and those facilities that meet the requisite standards and quality of services also form part of the facilities for international tourists (see Chapter 6). Rao and Suresh (2001: 207–208) have also recognised that '[t]he rush of [domestic] tourists has begun to pose problems for the police, the municipality, transport management, parking and waste disposal agencies, and disrupts the life of the residents who are not offering accommodation or other services to tourism'. They conclude that '[a]s long as demand assessment is based on international tourists and first class domestic tourists, the mass of middle-level and low-cost demand will continue to put pressure on the established destinations'. Indeed, the sustainability of domestic tourism in the face of global changes is something that will require further research in the future. The next chapter focuses on the related tourism experiences of India's diaspora as well as wider tourism mobilities in the Indian context.

# 8 Tourism mobilities and India's diaspora

## Introduction

The concept of mobility has now become an evocative keyword for the twenty-first century and encompasses both the large-scale movements of people, objects, capital and information across the world, and the more local processes of daily transportation, movement through public space and the travel of material things within everyday life (Sheller and Urry, 2004; Urry, 2007; Hannam *et al.*, 2006). As Sheller and Urry (2004: 1) write in their book *Tourism Mobilities*:

> We refer to 'tourism mobilities', then, not simply to state the obvious (that tourism is a form of mobility), but to highlight that many different mobilities inform tourism, shape the places where tourism is performed, and drive the making and unmaking of tourist destinations. Mobilities of people and objects, airplanes and suitcases, plants and animals, images and brands, data systems and satellites, all go into 'doing' tourism. . . . Tourism mobilities involve complex combinations of movement and stillness, realities and fantasies, play and work.

Thus, dreams of 'hyper-mobility' and 'instantaneous communication' have arguably driven contemporary tourism business strategies, marketing and policies while also eliciting strong political critique from those who may feel marginalised or otherwise affected by new tourism developments (Hannam *et al.*, 2006). Hence, in this chapter, the study of *tourism mobilities* will discuss the many interconnections between tourism and the wider movement of people in terms of migration and India's diaspora; between tourism and different modes of transport use in terms of infrastructures; between tourism and means of communicating in terms of new technological developments; and between tourism and the movement of material things such as food in the context of the Indian diaspora.

More often than not these tourism mobilities become more evident during times of crisis. For instance, when we have an outbreak of a particular disease this raises fears of mobilities and the associated risks increasingly determine logics of tourism governance (see Box 8.1 and Chapter 2). Tourism mobilities are thus

---

**Box 8.1  The effects of the 1994 plague outbreak in India**

In August 1994, an outbreak of bubonic plague was reported from the Beed district, a known plague-enzootic region in Maharashtra State in western India. In late September, news came of an explosive epidemic of suspected primary pneumonic plague in the city of Surat in neighboring Gujarat State. Hundreds of suspected cases and more than 50 deaths were reported from Surat. Press accounts described a mass exodus of hundreds of thousands of persons from this industrialized port city of nearly 2 million inhabitants. By early October, more than 6300 suspected cases of plague had been reported from 12 Indian states, including Delhi, but only a few were considered laboratory confirmed, primarily by unvalidated serologic techniques.
. . .

The initial reports of the outbreak caused considerable international concern about the risk for exportation of pneumonic plague from India. Official responses in various countries ranged from the enhancement of surveillance for ill travelers arriving at airports to the closure of borders, the embargo of flights to and from India, and the restriction of imports of Indian goods. Commerce between the United States and India, however, remained unrestricted during the epidemic. By enhancing surveillance at airports, providing written information about plague to all air travelers arriving from abroad, and promptly disseminating information on plague to clinicians and health department personnel, health officials in this country identified and evaluated for plague 13 travelers who had recently arrived from India with febrile illnesses and other conditions (CDC. Unpublished data). Two persons were found to have malaria, one had both dengue and malaria, and one had *Salmonella* bacteremia. No tourists in India are known to have contracted plague, and no patients with plague are known to have departed India during the crisis. The economic costs of emergency response systems implemented internationally during this crisis undoubtedly were substantial, and the resulting losses to the Indian tourism industry and other industries are expected to be staggering.

(Campbell and Hughes, 1995: 151–153)

---

centrally involved in reorganising institutions, generating climate change, moving risks and illnesses across the globe, altering travel, tourism and migration patterns, producing a more distant family life, transforming the social and educational life of young people, connecting distant people through so-called 'weak ties' and so on. However, such mobilities cannot be described without attention to the necessary spatial, infrastructural and institutional *moorings* or places that configure and enable mobilities (Hannam *et al.*, 2006). As we have discussed in Chapter 2, airports are a good example of platforms that enable these diverse mobilities.

Tesfahuney (1998: 501) writes that: '[d]ifferential mobility empowerments reflect structures and hierarchies of power and position by race, gender, age and class, ranging from the local to the global'. Rights to travel, for example, are highly uneven and skewed even between a single pair of countries (see Timothy, 2001; Gogia, 2006). As we shall see, different types of tourists may have different mobility empowerments. The tourist from India visiting England may have very different entitlements from the tourist from England, Germany or France visiting India.

## Conceptualising tourism and human mobilities

From this perspective, the analysis of tourism, then, needs to be (re)positioned within a broader context of human mobility. For example, we need to ask questions of how and when tourists become migrants for instance. The relations between outmigration, return migration, transnationalism and tourism need to be investigated in the Indian context. In their recent edited collection, Williams and Hall (2002: 2) have noted how, in the contemporary world, political, technological, financial and transportational changes have been critical in significantly lowering the barriers to mobility for many. As a result, new forms of mobility have been increasingly taken up by both younger and older adults:

> Those who first experience tourism and travel as children, are probably more likely to become independent youth travellers, and then to take their own children on holiday, and finally to become well-travelled elderly people. Each round of tourism and travel, at different points in the life course, extends direct experience of particular places and general familiarity with tourism. This in turn establishes the knowledge base and the expectations that will sustain high levels of mobility in later stages of the life course.
>
> (Williams and Hall, 2002: 14–15)

And, of course, these changes are taking place in India. As we shall see, the growing Indian middle class is not content with domestic tourism and is increasingly seeking destinations abroad to visit. Moreover, the vast Indian diaspora takes an active part in 'managing' these connections. Moreover, studies of migration, diasporas and transnational citizenship offer trenchant critiques of the bounded and static categories of nation, ethnicity, community, place and state within much social science (Brah, 1996; Gilroy, 1993; Joseph, 1999; Ong, 1999). These works, drawn not only from the social sciences but also from literary and cultural studies, highlight dislocation, displacement, disjuncture and dialogism as widespread conditions of migrant-tourist subjectivity and 'nomadism' in the world today (see D'Andrea, 2006; Hannam, 2008). At the same time, they also foreground acts of 'homing' (Brah, 1996; Fortier, 2000) and 'regrounding' (Ahmed *et al.*, 2003) that point towards the complex inter-relation between travel and dwelling. Indeed, as we shall see, in leaving a place, migrant-tourists often carry parts of their home with them, which are reassembled in the material form of souvenirs, textures, foods, colours, scents and sounds – reconfiguring the place of arrival both figuratively and imaginatively (Tolia-Kelly, 2006; see Chapter 4). And migrants frequently return home to visit friends and relatives while being ostensibly 'on holiday' in their country of origin (O'Reilly, 2000; Duval, 2003; Coles and Timothy, 2004).

We can see this most pertinently in relation to tourism and diaspora populations. In Barber's (2001: 178) definition diasporas are 'communities that define themselves by reference to a distant homeland from which they once originated'. Such diasporas tend to make important connections back to their places of origin (despite, and often because of, their many displacements) in terms of tourism. In their book *Tourism, Diasporas and Space*, Coles and Timothy (2004: 19) 'focus on three sets of themes which are beginning to emerge in tourism studies of diaspora: namely, diaspora experiences of tourism; the spaces occupied by diaspora tourists; and the production of tourism for and by diasporic communities'. They go on to discuss how diaspora identities are creolised or hybridised (Lowe, 1991; Featherstone, 1995; Friedmann, 1999).

On the one hand, forms of diaspora tourism may be seen as voyages of self-discovery and identity affirmation 'in search of their roots'. This search for roots has also manifested itself in the rise of so-called 'genealogical' (Nash, 2002; Meethan, 2004; Basu, 2007), 'ancestral' (S. Fowler, 2003) or 'family history' (Timothy and Guelke, 2008) tourism. On the other hand, however, visits to diasporic homelands may result in troubling, disconcerting and ambiguous experiences as well as new-found ambivalences (Stephenson, 2002; Duval, 2003; Hannam, 2004c). Perhaps more interesting, however, is how diasporic communities can lead to the production of new forms of tourism as they become visited themselves by residents of the original 'homeland'. As Coles and Timothy (2004: 43) argue, 'Residents of the original "homeland" may make a trip to diaspora spaces to discover how co-members of the diaspora, perhaps even their friends and relations, have adapted to life and conditions in another place'. In so doing, they may make trips to view sites of heritage, which may take the form of so-called 'dark tourism' (as in sites associated with the death of ancestors), or trips that take the form of engaging with specific destinations, festivals and events targeted specifically at them (see Chapters 3 and 4). The point we would like to make is that a diasporic population has been key to the development of outbound tourism from India. Moreover, as part of contemporary urban development strategies, many diasporic communities have become the object of a wider tourist gaze. For example, many tourists of all backgrounds visit the many 'Little Indias' that can be found in major world cities. Such ethnic districts are redefined as tourist destinations for 'they have acquired a new historical and sentimental salience in the post-modern developmental era' (Lin, 1995: 629). McKercher and Du Cros (2002: 131) define 'ethnic tourism' as 'emphasising the otherness of a place in terms of the tourist's frame of reference'. However, not all ethnic districts offer cultural activities or a tangible heritage. In this case, many visitors come for the atmosphere, to shop and to consume food and drink. The ethnicity of the community may appear as an exotic backdrop but the original idea of meeting the 'Other' turns into a purely commercial exchange. In some cases, it goes so far that ethnic districts lose their community focus and are transformed into wholly commodified tourist attractions providing food and other business (Conforti, 1996; Diekmann and Maulet, 2009). Hence, through tourism development, sites such as Brick Lane in London or Little India in Singapore have become alienated from their original community to become hyped Asian dining areas (Chang, 1999).

We now turn to an examination of India's diaspora to exemplify this further. The Indian diaspora has been the subject of a great deal of empirical research in recent years because of its diversity and complexity. This needs to be placed in the context of India's foreign policies and attempts by the Indian government to overtly engage with the Indian diaspora (see also Chapter 2). The idea of the diaspora being a 'hidden asset' in terms of its economic potential was not taken seriously by the Indian government until the late 1990s. In particular, we want to evaluate India's recent tourism policies, which have been aimed at bringing the Indian diaspora back to India as tourists. But then we also look at how, conversely, India's diaspora has become involved in marketing other destinations as sites for India's outbound tourists to visit.

We will discuss how India's relationship both with its diaspora and with its tourism industry is at best ambivalent. This is in direct contrast to other developing countries where there has been much more positive, enthusiastic and proactive engagement with their respective diasporas for reasons including income generation and place promotion, and nation building. There are several probable reasons for this. First of all, India has failed to engage with its diaspora historically, which has led to some disaffection amongst the Indian diaspora. Furthermore, research suggests that second and third generations of the Indian diaspora have been ambivalent about returning to India; they would rather utilise family networks than engage directly with the Indian government and its attempts to reach out to them directly through marketing and promotions. Finally, the complexity of the regional, ethnic and religious divisions within and among the Indian diaspora largely frustrates a unified approach towards India's diaspora.

## India's diaspora

The Indian diaspora is estimated at between 14 and 20 million people worldwide, which is relatively small in comparison with other diasporas such as the Chinese and small given the size of the Indian population as a whole. Indian migrants can be found all over the world; however, there are major concentrations in the Gulf region, the United States, Britain and Canada (Varma, 2004). Based upon previous research, five major groups of migrants within the Indian diaspora have been identified (Clarke *et al.*, 1990). First, there are emigrants who left India under the British colonial system (R. Cohen, 1997), for example indentured labourers and migrants who travelled (often under duress) to South-East Asia, Africa, the Caribbean and Polynesia up to 1930s to work in the plantations of the British, French and Dutch colonies (Varma, 2004). The second group comprises commercial migrants who left India for Africa, Australia, Europe and the Americas just before and immediately after independence (circa 1920–60). Low- and high-skilled migrants who left India for short-term contract work in the Middle East from the 1970s onwards constitute the third group. Fourth, there are the so called 'brain drain' migrants who left India for higher education and better jobs in the United Kingdom, the United States, Canada and, largely from the 1980s onwards, Australia. Finally, there have been migrants to other parts of the South Asian subcontinent (notably Pakistan and Bangladesh) in the aftermath of independence. Some of these migrants have maintained their Indian citizenship, some of them have acquired the nationality of their host society, but most have maintained at least informal links with the country of their origin (Lall, 2001). Varma (2004: 200) explains that:

> Non-resident Indians (NRIs) were until recently derisively called 'Non-Required Indians'; a vague sense of guilt clung to them for having deserted the country; their motherland had little use for them; and they in turn, were embarrassed by her poverty and backwardness.

Van der Veer (1995), meanwhile, has highlighted the considerable hostility in the United States towards recent Indian immigrants. After 1965 US immigration laws restricted migration to those with professional skills, business interests or sizeable amounts of capital to invest. However, interestingly, Van der Veer argues that the Indian diaspora in the United States maintains a continuing interest in its roots; that is, the search for an elusive and largely mythical India. Meanwhile, in her research, Lessinger (1999) argues that Indian migrants in America construct new hybrid identities for themselves, combining as they do elements of Indian-ness and elements of American-ness. She also notes that 'most immigrants are slightly defensive about having left India, for which all retain strong, if ambivalent, emotions' (Lessinger 1999: 20). The vast South Asian diaspora literature, by authors such as Jhumpa Lahiri or Monica Ali, very often exploits this conflict between Indian traditional values and the 'modern' Western world in their novels (for a critical review see Ghosh, 2003). Moreover, many Bollywood films also highlight these differences further (see also Chapter 3).

In the UK context Bhachu (1999: 71) has researched the multiple migratory experiences of British Punjabi women. She has argued that South Asian women's 'marriage and dowry patterns are, like their identities, continuously negotiated and determined not by their migration histories but powerfully filtered through by the codes of their local and national cultures and also by their class positions' (Bhachu, 1999: 71). Moreover, 'those who have emigrated more than once possess very powerful communication networks which have been greatly facilitated and enhanced by global communications' (Bhachu, 1999: 72). This research has also demonstrated that the Indian diaspora is internally riven with complex and multifarious fractures, and is hence extremely heterogeneous. Groups within the Indian diaspora have had a variety of different historical trajectories, and have developed in widely divergent historical contexts in many parts of the world (Van der Veer, 1995). It is the fragmented nature of these contexts and experiences that complicates the idea of an Indian diaspora. The differences within the Indian diaspora derive from political and geographical origins (India, Pakistan and Bangladesh), often in combination with religious and ethnic schisms (Hindu, Muslim, Sikh, Buddhist, Christian, etc.). In turn, this is overlaid with both linguistic and economic divisions (Bhardwaj and Madhusudana Rao, 1990). In this context, Ghosh (2003: 265) argues that 'India exported with her population, not a language, as other civilizations have done, but a linguistic process – the process of adaptation to heteroglossia'. Moreover, the sense of national consciousness varies from region to region, and it is often specific regions to which individual expatriate Indians remain attached (Lall, 2001).

In spite of these complex fractures in Indian society and culture, it has been argued that the Indian migratory experience can actually lead to a stronger sense of identity on the margins of the host society. Thus:

> those who do not think of themselves as Indians before migration become Indians in the diaspora. The element of romanticization which is present in every nationalism is even stronger among nostalgic migrants, who often form a rosy picture of the country they have left and are able to imagine the nation where it did not exist before.
>
> (Van der Veer, 1995: 7)

Each diaspora constitutes a multiple weaving of many disparate narratives of identity. However, at times these may come together in a confluence of narratives as the experience of diaspora is lived and relived. As Brah (1996: 196) has argued, 'diasporic identities are at once local and global. They are networks of transnational identifications encompassing "imagined" and "encountered" communities'.

When India gained independence in 1947, the Nehru government's foreign policy excluded the issue of expatriate Indians from policy formulation and actively encouraged the Indian diaspora to integrate into their host societies. According to Lall (2001: 41), 'In Nehru's eyes the expatriate Indians had forfeited their Indian citizenship and identity by moving abroad and did not need the support of their mother country'. Nehru had made expatriate Indians alien in a legal sense, and this position had several drawbacks. First, it meant that India could not get involved when part of the diaspora was going through political, economic or social discrimination (Bahadur Singh, 1979). Second, despite continuing informal ties between members of the diaspora and their families in their places of origin, the diaspora was not encouraged to take part directly in the economic development of India.

Rajiv Gandhi's politics in the 1980s, however, heralded a new era in which the potential of the NRI was actively discussed. In particular, two new categories of the Indian diaspora (temporary workers in the Middle East and the highly educated economic migrants in the West) brought about a renewed government interest in the diaspora. These new categories of NRIs made substantial money and maintained informal family ties in India. However, although India tried to facilitate opportunities for the remittances coming from the Gulf, it largely failed to open up the economy for any serious NRI investment beyond the family unit. Indeed, as previously mentioned, the diaspora became an interesting economic asset for the Indian government only in the late 1990s with the general opening of India's economy. After the end of the Cold War, liberalisation of the Indian economy brought with it fresh hope that the diaspora would invest heavily in the Indian economy. However, even after liberalisation, there was little the government was prepared to do to establish a formal relationship with diaspora communities and members (Lall, 2001). Successive governments remained suspicious of the latent power of the Indian diaspora. It was felt that the diaspora might attempt to corrupt the political system by buying votes in elections. Anti-globalisation protestors also felt that there was a threat that the diaspora would corrupt Indian culture. As Varma (2004: 200) states:

> Culture was the umbilical cord that held the two (motherland and NRIs) together; but in every other way they were on independent journeys, burrowing along tunnels of their own in the elusive search for prosperity. Today at the end of the tunnel, they are rediscovering each other.

Nevertheless, the novelist Amitav Ghosh (2003: 263) has argued that:

> The modern Indian diaspora – the huge migration from the subcontinent that began in the mid-nineteenth century – is not merely one of the most important demographic dislocations of modern times: it now represents an important force in world culture. The culture of the diaspora is also increasingly a factor within the culture of the Indian subcontinent.

It is important to think of the Indian diaspora in both these ways when we consider it in relation to tourism, first in terms of the impact that the Indian diaspora can make on inbound tourism (see also Chapter 6) and second in terms of the impact it can make on domestic outbound tourism (see also Chapter 7).

## India's inbound diaspora tourism

Since 2001, the High Level Committee on Indian Diaspora has made it known that the diaspora could make a significant contribution to the growth of tourism in India. This would be mainly in the form of providing the necessary investment for capital projects such as visitor attractions and resort complexes. In this light, the committee recommended that suitable schemes be devised both to attract members of the diaspora to India and to motivate PIO (persons of Indian origin) travel agents to promote tourism to India. The committee noted that first-generation visitors from the United Kingdom to India visit almost annually, subject to their financial status, whereas succeeding generations tend to limit their visits to important family occasions or tourism. This is reinforced by Leonard's research (1999: 47) in which it was noted that:

Second generation Hyderabadis abroad cheerfully told me that they had not liked Hyderabad at all when they visited it and saw no resemblance to the place described by their parents. Some who had not visited Hyderabad said they had the Taj at Agra and the historic buildings in Delhi on their list of places to visit ahead of Hyderabad. One organised visit of second generation youngsters from the United States was in some ways a disaster, filled with disappointed expectations and cultural misunderstandings: many of these youngsters said in the end that they preferred Bangalore. The homeland has in effect disappeared, so transformed that it is unrecognisable.

In spite of this evidence, the High Level Committee on Indian Diaspora has recommended that there should be a greater focus on promoting tourism among second-generation PIOs. It argued that special tour packages, pilgrim packages and packages tailor-made for this group of diaspora should be developed and publicised (Ministry of External Affairs, 2001).

The need to boost tourism was further recognised at a special session on 'Hospitality and Tourism: Branding Strategies for India' hosted by the Minister of Tourism in 2003. The Minister of Tourism argued that the Indian diaspora should contribute to marketing the right image of India overseas. He further argued that '[t]he government is making its best efforts to remove bottlenecks faced by the tourism industry and has decided to launch a special campaign *Discover India, Discover Yourself* for the Indians living abroad' (Rediff.com, 2003). In reality, however, many of the delegates were disappointed by their return to India for this event. In particular, the state of India's airports and national airline were heavily criticised (Sen, 2003). Many also felt that the regulations imposed on many returning diaspora members were draconian if they planned to stay for any length of time. These regulations included the requirement for an AIDS certificate and an income tax certificate, as well as a certificate to prove that they had not committed any crimes. Moreover, there were complaints of harassment at airports by customs officials. For example, Vetcha and Bhaskar (2003) cite the example of a man from England who was detained for twelve hours for bringing a television into India. It was argued that, despite paying customs duty, he was detained because he refused to bribe the officials and, as a direct consequence of this unfortunate event, he refused to return to India.

At present, however, the approach of the Indian government to the diaspora is contradictory; it is attempting to engage with its diaspora more explicitly and actively, but it remains by and large ambivalent, a somewhat distorted 'mirror in which modern India seeks to know itself' (Ghosh, 2003: 269). As we shall see, many diaspora members are equally ambivalent about returning to India as tourists. For many, a visit to India has become not so much a vacation as an homage to the extended family; a break from the ordinary, everyday world by observing familial piety elsewhere. Their visits tend to revolve around 'traditional' ancestral sites, although for second- and third-generation visitors the allure of other visitor attractions, destinations and resorts rather than familial locations is difficult to resist (Hannam, 2004c).

## India's outbound tourism

Many countries that host India's diaspora are also turning their attentions to tourism as they seek out new markets. Hence, we now turn to look at how these countries have sought to attract the 8.5 million outbound Indian tourists by providing an ethnic infrastructure. Over twenty countries have recently set up tourism promotion centres in India and we will focus first on the United Kingdom.

According to the UK government in 2006 there were 367,000 visits to the United Kingdom by Indian passport holders. The marketing agency for tourism in the United Kingdom, VisitBritain, expects visits from India to increase significantly in future years and regards India as a 'priority emerging market'. In 2006 it was reported that for the first time Indian tourists spent more in the United Kingdom than Japanese tourists – 'underling the scale of the emerging middle class and the strength of the Indian economy' (Finch, 2007). The average spend by an Indian tourist is £793 compared with £710 by an American tourist. Nearly half of all Indian visitors to Britain now come from the smaller Indian cities such as Pune. Moreover, in 2007, VisitBritain launched a map of Bollywood film locations in the United Kingdom to attract more tourists from India. Significantly, it launched this at the International Indian Film Academy Awards (IIFA) ceremony in Yorkshire (the second time it had been held in the UK; see Box 8.2). Monika Mohta, Director, Nehru Centre and Minister of Culture at the Indian High Commission argues that:

> Indians will go to see the same movie countless times, so sights such as Windsor Castle and Buckingham Palace become very familiar, virtually embedded in their minds . . . Tower Bridge is in practically every second Bollywood film. Many cinema-goers aspire to be able to say that they've been to the same places as their icons.
>
> (Apunkachoice.com, 2007)

However, this mediatised tourist experience is still predicated on there being an Indian diaspora in the United Kingdom that has developed an ethnic infrastructure to support Indian visitors.

Ireland, meanwhile, has also recently begun to target India as a source of tourists by laying on free familiarisation tours of Ireland for Indian tour operators. Tourism Ireland research has shown that the key reasons why visitors from 'new and developing' markets such as India wish to visit Ireland are the friendliness of the people, the beauty of the scenery and the cultural and heritage experiences on offer here (Tourism Ireland, 2009). Like VisitBritain, Tourism Ireland has undertaken considerable groundwork in India and has established an office in Mumbai. In May 2009, the major Indian tour operator Cox & Kings included Dublin in one of its most popular European itineraries for the first time ever.

Looking elsewhere in Europe, Spain has also begun to 'woo niche Indian tourists' by improving air connectivity, easing visa regulations and opening an office in Mumbai. In Finland, they now expect some 70,000 Indian tourists and they

**Box 8.2  IIFA film awards**

The IIFA Awards have been established to recognize, honour and celebrate the achievements of the Indian film industry in the arena of world cinema.

The IIFA Awards evening is a glamorous stage production combining the best of Indian and international entertainment. As a prelude to the awards the media are treated to a red carpet special as the walk out in glitz and glamour giving the world media a glimpse of what beholds.

IIFA celebrates India Cinema across the world. As global cinema rapidly emerges, a prominent place for Indian Cinema is reserved. IIFA constantly endeavours to showcase to the world the wealth of talent Indian Cinema has to offer. Year on year, each IIFA experience is even more stunning than the one before.

From its inception, IIFA has been creating bonds . . . between people, between film industries, between countries. Starting with a venue as defining as the Millennium Dome, on the outskirts of London, IIFA fever gripped the world. During the week of IIFA, Indian Cinema was news on the hour across all television channels. The London Times headline screamed: 'Move Over LA. Here Comes Mumbai.' . . . In the subsequent years, the IIFA Awards grew from a one-night event into a three-day Weekend, wherein the IIFA Awards are the highlight.

Wherever IIFA has left its mark, it has promoted the business of Indian Cinema and provided it an impetus. The sale of tickets of Hindi cinema grew by thirty five percent in the UK in the six months after IIFA. In South Africa, Hindi films moved from matinee shows on weekends to mainline theatres and now there are competing distribution chains vying for the rights to exhibit Hindi films across Africa. In Malaysia, there was an increase in the value of rights for Indian Cinema and the collection from exhibition and sale of non-pirated DVDs increased by more than 50 percent. The number of Indian visitors to Malaysia has risen by 35 percent and Indian occupancy at Genting Highlands rose by 190 percent in the year after IIFA. In 2004, the doors were opened for Indian filmmakers to film in Singapore.

The IIFA Movement continues . . .

(http://www.iifa.com/web07/cntnt/aboutiifa-indianfilmindustry.htm)

have drafted plans to promote the Finnish countryside as a location for the filming of Bollywood films to try and compete with Switzerland (see Box 8.3 and Figure 8.1). Even Monaco has jumped on this bandwagon; as a luxury, high-end destination it wished to attract high-spending Indian tourists to Monaco by encouraging the opening of more Indian restaurants and possibly bringing a Bollywood production to the principality (Porter, 2007).

Outside of Europe, Singapore has also sought Indian tourists recently, with the Singapore Tourist Board aiming to get Indian tourists to visit Singapore 'not just

---

**Box 8.3 Switzerland to woo India with Bollywood film locations tourism campaign**

There has long been a connection between India and Switzerland, but until now, that connection has been a cinematic one. As many films, especially Yash Raj films, have been shot at least in part in Switzerland, usually a song or two.

Now the European ski destination is attempting to not only woo Indian films, but also its travelers.

A series of adverts have been sponsored by Switzerland Tourism, the city of Lucerne, and Kuoni Travels' Indian operation encouraging Indians to 'experience the magic' and take a break in some of the regions seen in some India's most famous films, such as the iconic Yash Raj Film *Darr*, which was shot on location in Switzerland.

Suhel Seth, managing director of Counselage, a brand and marketing consultancy said that it is not longer impossible for Indians experince the locations in these films, now they '. . . can be part of the scene by going there'.

Yash Raj Films recently joined SOTC, an arm of the Kuoni Travel Group in India, to provide tours in Switzerland for film fans. YRF Enchanted Journey offers a tour of locations used by Yash Raj Films in some of its hits, including *Dilwale Dulhania Le Jayenge*, *Mohabbatein*, *Veer-Zaara*, *Chandni*, *Darr* and *Bachna Ae Haseeno*.

(http://allbollywood.com/ab/news/2010/0305/485838/yash-chopra/)

---

for holidays but for meetings, company retreats, honeymoon getaways, school trips and family outings' (*Thaindian News*, 2008). Tourism Malaysia is promoting itself to the Indian market as a golf destination with special packages. Bali recently saw a large increase in the number of Indian tourists visiting – an 81 per cent jump up to 19,000 visitors. The Philippines, meanwhile, has started an aggressive campaign to lure Indian tourists, many of whom do not know where the Philippines is geographically (Uy, 2007). Vietnam has also decided to get in on the act with plans to launch roadshows aimed at top-end Indian tourists and by giving Bollywood producers incentives to film in Vietnam in an effort to change Indian tourists' negative perceptions of their country. Mauritius, with its sizeable Indian diaspora, has also begun to offer discount packages to attract Indian tourists. More Indian tourists are also heading to Dubai to take advantage of its shopping facilities. Egypt has also begun the hard sell, arguing that it is cheaper and more attractive than other destinations, focusing in its marketing on the historical ties between the two countries and pointing out that Egypt caters to the Indian taste in terms of culture, religion, entertainment and shopping experiences. With the Indian Premier League (IPL) cricket currently being held in South Africa, South Africa has not been shy about trying to market its country as a destination for the Indian tourist. South Africa has an extensive Indian diasporic infrastructure and

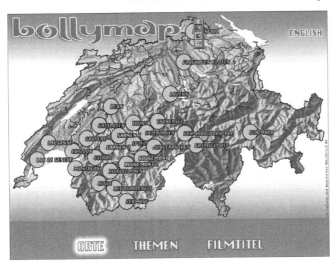

*Figure 8.1* Bollymap.

rather than go for the high-end middle-aged market it has targeted the 'twenty-somethings' that like to have a good time. Finally, Australia hopes to become the next hotspot for Indian tourists following a Baz Luhrmann-designed campaign.

## India's tourism mobilities

As we noted at the beginning of this chapter the mobilities concept involves not just human mobility, but the interconnections between this and other aspects of mobility – infrastructural, technological and material. In what follows we consider each of these in turn.

In terms of infrastructures, we need to recognise how India has developed new ways of moving both people and things around the country, as well as into and out of the country. Many international tourists arrive in India by plane at one of its international airports. In response to widespread criticism of the state of India's airports, in the late 1990s India embarked upon a large-scale airport renovation and development programme. This involved the formation of the

> Airports Authority of India (AAI) on the 1st April 1995 by merging the International Airports Authority of India and the National Airports Authority with a view to accelerate the integrated development, expansion and modernisation of the operational, terminal and cargo facilities at the airports in the country conforming to international standards.
>
> (AAI, 2010)

In her book *Managing Airports*, Anne Graham (2008) notes that this heralded a new era of private investment in India's airports, although the Indian government retains at least 26 per cent ownership. In particular, two new airports were developed at the key IT centres of Bangalore and Hyderabad, with significant investment from Switzerland and Malaysia, respectively, while other key airports in Delhi and Mumbai have also been substantially upgraded with extensive private investment (Figure 8.2).

After experiencing the airport, the next form of infrastructural mobility that tourists face is India's roads. Again, these have previously been highly criticised as being in a poor state of repair. Nevertheless, the engagement with India's roads is a key part of the tourist experience. As Edensor (2002: 120) writes of driving in India, it 'is necessary to sound your horn to warn a vehicle that you wish to overtake, for rear view mirrors are rarely used and often absent'. Moreover, the near constant traffic congestion in urban areas with people, animals, carts, buses, bicycles and increasing numbers of cars sharing the road disrupts the Western concept of the road as a way to progress linearly from 'a' to 'b' and provides what Edensor (2002: 121) calls a 'fluid choreography'. Similarly, as we have seen in previous chapters, the experience of India's railways is also an important aspect of contemporary tourism mobilities in India – including the high-class Palace on Wheels, the everyday experience of a backpacker booking a reservation for a sleeper train from Delhi and the heritage 'toy' trains in the Himalayas (see Box 8.4).

*Figure 8.2* Mumbai domestic airport.

---

**Box 8.4  The Darjeeling Himalayan Railway Society**

The Darjeeling Himalayan Railway Society is an International group, based in the UK, dedicated to promoting awareness of, interest in, and support for, The Darjeeling Himalayan Railway, India.

The DHR Society was founded by a small band of concerned enthusiasts in 1997, who, aware of the railways uncertain state, decided to be active and form a focus for all those who are interested in the line and are concerned for its future.

With a membership of over 800 in 24 countries the DHRS seeks to appeal to those who may, have an interest in the area, or merely this remarkable line, whether it is of an historical nature, more contemporary history or even to 'model it'.

(http://www.dhrs.org/dhrs_main_page.htm)

---

In terms of technological mobility, tourists visiting India have previously found the experience a fairly immobile one until recently, with letters marked *poste restante* arriving at post offices some weeks after they have been sent from the West. However, India has been at the forefront of the revolution into the use of new mobile telephone and internet technologies in the twenty-first century, with current estimates of a 'tele-density' of 44 per cent of the population having a mobile phone – over 500 million subscribers (Bhaumik, 2010). Abraham (2007) discusses, for example, how mobile phone use has transformed many fishing communities in Kerala, which have now diversified into the tourism industry. Srivastava (2005), meanwhile, notes that the virtual domestic tourist is now able to send prayers by SMS to various shrine sites in India. International tourists, on the other hand, are able to also send SMS messages back 'home' and thus the dislocation they perhaps previously experienced in India is now mitigated. International tourists also frequent the ubiquitous internet cafe – an enclavic space – to send photos home and chat online with fellow travellers (see Paris, 2010). Nevertheless, tourists and locals still rely on the ISD booths to make calls back home as mobile phone technology remains costly, particularly for the backpacker market (Figure 8.3).

In terms of material mobility, again tourism has historically been highly involved. If we reflect on the mobility of food, clearly we can immediately recognise the impact of Indian food culture and cuisine around the world. Arjun Appadurai (1988) has discussed, in this context, how many cookbooks written for Western audiences tell unusual tales about India and its cuisine. Moreover, for the Indian diaspora, food plays an important part in shaping memories of India and the 'myth of return'. As Mankekar (2005: 204) notes, Indian food 'enables the reproduction of "culture" in the diaspora'. For many tourists, eating Indian food may serve as a motivation for visiting India (although many Western restaurants serve an anglicised–Bangladeshi hybrid, Indian cuisine is the most popular

*Figure 8.3* ISD booth, New Delhi.

cuisine in the United Kingdom). However, this motivation is often then disrupted by the actual experience of eating in India and the contraction of so-called 'Delhi belly'. Nevertheless, the point we wish to make is that food is a key aspect of India's tourism mobilities; it flows around the world and is an important aspect of the touristic experience.

**Box 8.5  The Musée Guimet, Paris**

The Musée Guimet was the brain-child of Emile Guimet (1836–1918), a Lyons industrialist who devised the grand project of opening a museum devoted to the religions of Ancient Egypt, Classical Antiquity, and Asia. Guimet visited Egypt and Greece before traveling around the world in 1876, stopping off in Japan, China and India. In the course of his travels he acquired extensive collections of objects which he put on display in a museum opened in Lyon in 1879. These collections were subsequently transferred to a new museum which he had built in Paris and which was inaugurated ten years later, in 1889. During Emile Guimet's own lifetime, the museum, while maintaining a section devoted to the religions of Ancient Egypt, increasingly focused on Asian civilizations.

(http://www.guimet.fr/History-of-the-museum)

Similarly, we can also note the importance of shopping and the purchase of souvenirs as a material mobile practice of the touristic encounter with India – something we have discussed in depth in Chapter 4. Indeed, when it comes to understanding India's heritage, many Western tourists first view India's heritage in the various museums located in the West – such museums being repositories of material Indian artefacts that were accumulated and transported to the West during the colonial period and which are now politically contested sites of material mobility (see Box 8.5).

## Conclusions

In conclusion, this chapter has discussed the role that India's diaspora makes in terms of inbound tourism to India. It has also examined the ambivalent role of the Indian government in promoting India as both a destination and a site of investment for the Indian diaspora. It has then examined the role of the Indian diaspora as an ethnic infrastructure for India's growing outbound tourism market. Finally, this chapter has sought to provide a critical and reflexive introduction to understanding the diverse tourism mobilities that occur with(in) India. Overall, however, it is somewhat startling that there is so little critical contemporary research into these various aspects of India's tourism mobilities – something we will return to in our final chapter, which develops a future research agenda for tourism and India.

# 9  Concluding thoughts

A research agenda for tourism and India

## Introduction

This book aimed to draw together insights into India's relationship with tourism and to add to the relatively small corpus of academic literature on tourism and India. As highlighted in several chapters in this book, India as a tourist destination has not yet attracted broad attention from the international tourism scholarly community. In comparison with tourism research on other developing countries, relatively few papers on India have been published in international tourism journals and there are very few books that specifically deal critically with India's tourism issues. Indian scholars' publications, meanwhile, often address the Indian public rather than an international audience and do not benefit from a wide distribution. Therefore, we have attempted to pull together the various books and articles that have been published to provide the reader with a 'state of the art' commentary on tourism and India. In this concluding chapter we wish to first provide a brief summary of the book by noting some of the significant connections between previous chapters. We then go on to discuss recent developments in terms of India's tourism promotion, before finally outlining a research agenda for tourism and India in the twenty-first century.

## Tourism and India: a summary

Chapter 6 on international travel and tourism to India analysed the historical relationship between India and its British rulers to explore the romantic views that were largely diffused through orientalist constructions. This chapter also explored the first intercultural contacts that many Western travellers had with India, and in many ways these travel accounts continue to perpetrate the exotic image of the country for Western travellers. For many independent travellers in particular, visiting India from the 1980s onwards was considered to be a rite of passage. In terms of the international market, contemporary India is now trying to shed its older image as a 'traveller' destination by positioning itself as a destination for new forms of tourism and in particular medical tourism. One of the reasons for the success of India as a medical tourism destination is the quality of the health care provided to international patients. Indeed, Indian medical staff are sometimes educated in Western universities and this also connects to India as a diasporic tourist destination, as highlighted in Chapter 8. Moreover, there is a vast Indian diaspora around the world, with significant concentrations in the Middle East and various Commonwealth countries, particularly the United Kingdom, Canada and the United States. The members of the diaspora constitute a huge potential market for India's tourism industry and specific campaigns have recently been launched by the Indian tourism authorities to address this group in particular. We showed in Chapter 3, for example, the importance of Bollywood for this diaspora tourism and how the Indian film industry participates in the spreading of Indian cultural values to different migrant generations through the content of the films.

Moreover, throughout many of the chapters in this book the role of the burgeoning Indian middle class in further tourism development has been evident. In Chapter 6, for example, we highlighted the creation of theme parks, such as Rajasthani villages, that seek to recreate a rural environment for urban Indian visitors. Hence, it should not be forgotten that India's domestic market is extremely important, with over half a billion people travelling throughout the country – emphasising the significance of India's increasingly mobile population. Thus, in Chapter 7 we explored the multiple forms of pilgrimage-related tourism. Although the needs and expectations, travel means and accommodation preferences vary strongly between the domestic and international markets, it is interesting to see how the international tourism supply might influence the domestic tourism supply as the Indian middle class picks up on more international tourism traits.

This book has also discussed particular forms of tourism such as the rather controversial slum tourism in which mainly Western middle-class tourists visit some of the poorest communities in India. Without necessarily judging it, we have tried to analyse the motivations and experiences of some of these visitors. Tourists have highlighted the demand for a socially constructed 'authentic' experience to discover the 'real' India, which draws upon earlier orientalist romantic imagery, very much the opposite of the aforementioned 'staging' of the Rajastahani village theme park, although both provide a commodified experience. Moreover, another example in which the conceptions and perceptions of tourism lead to a conflict between domestic and foreign visitors is at the various heritage sites in India. In Chapter 4 we have thus debated the different use of and attitudes towards heritage sites and the different meanings these sites have for different groups. Indeed, the development of tourism in India is strongly linked to its colonial past – not only in terms of the governmental organisation of tourism in the country but also in terms of some of the key tourism features on offer. States such as Rajasthan and Himachal Pradesh have drawn their tourism potential from sites that have been either valorised (the maharaja's hotel palaces in Rajasthan) or constructed (Shimla's colonial architecture) under colonial rule. As pointed out in both Chapters 3 and 7, these tourism features also dwell on romantic and orientalist views but they are also key destinations for the Indian middle classes. Similarly, Chapter 5 has demonstrated how colonial rule impacted on the creation of India's system of national parks, which are presently major tourist destinations, in particular for domestic tourists.

## Furthering brand India

Nevertheless, having analysed the tourism policies and developments in India in previous chapters, a fundamental question perhaps remains: Why is there – compared with many other countries – so little international tourism in India? Many researchers think that India's share in world tourism is quite below its capacities (Chaudhary, 2000; Ravichandran and Suresh, 2010). As previously mentioned, India has been more engaged with the international tourism market since the beginning of the 1990s and has a vast number of potential cultural, heritage and environmental tourism sites to offer the contemporary tourist. Yet it ranks only forty-second on the UNWTO world destination list. There are, perhaps, no clear answers, but a wide variety of factors may help to answer this question. These elements can be divided into two categories: external factors not necessarily related to tourism and internal factors directly related to tourism.

External factors include terrorist attacks and threats, communal political and religious troubles, and, at a broader level, economic crises and outbreaks of serious diseases. Dhariwal (2005: 197), who analysed the importance of domestic disorders for tourism between 1996 and 2000 – thus before the two major crises of 9/11 and 28/11 – has stated that 'political disorder in India does have a negative impact on the international perspective and leads to significant decline of the tourist arrivals . . . . The disturbances due to terrorism and political instability emerge as the most significant factor deterring tourism growth'. Chaudhary (2000) confirms this picture, but believes it to be exaggerated and that India deserves a better image than that of mysticism, political instability, grinding poverty, illiteracy and communal discord. However, in his research conclusions he states that India lacks a positive image mainly in terms of a lack of basic infrastructure and as a generally 'unsafe' destination. Moreover, fears of health problems – due to poor sanitation – are probably more valid for India than for other countries, with international films such as *Slumdog Millionaire* reinforcing this image. But it is not only about these images of the country; there remains a lack of awareness by local hosts about the needs of international visitors.

In terms of internal factors related to tourism, India is, in comparison with other Asian countries, a rather expensive destination for many high-end international travellers (Capella-Cervera and Priestley, 2008). Luxury hotels can charge as much as in Western countries, whereas hotels in some other Asian countries charge much lower prices. The visual impression of urban as well as rural spaces is too often connected with filth and poverty. With 400 million people below the poverty line, health issues, violence and child- and gender-related issues continue to negatively affect the image of the South Asian region, including India (de Alwis, 2010). Travel from India's newly refurbished and modernised airports to luxury hotels also often challenges the comfort zones of many international visitors.

Being the largest democracy in the world with a highly complex system of governance, India's tourism management is also rather complicated, with very wide-ranging responsibilities for the central Ministry of Tourism. Since the 1990s India has begun to open up to the world in general, with a focus on international tourism replacing some of the earlier emphasis on nation building through domestic tourism. One important step has been the reaction of the Indian Ministry of Tourism to the drop in international tourist numbers in 2002 following the terrorist attacks of 9/11. Clearly, these attacks had an impact not only on tourism to India, but also on worldwide travel and tourism. India, however, used this occasion to build a new image of the country by creating a new brand – 'Incredible India' (see Chapter 2). Moreover, as in 2002 after the 9/11 crisis, following the November 2008 terrorist attacks in Mumbai the Ministry of Tourism developed a series of new actions to be taken to restore tourism to India – even as the sites of the attacks have become tourist sights themselves (Figure 9.1). M. Nayar (2009) notes that these actions included a 'rescue package' involving further international tourism marketing, tax breaks and subsidies for hotels.

In terms of furthering brand development, meanwhile, the current annual report of the Ministry of Tourism in India notes the importance of online marketing activities as part of its integrated marketing strategy. Moreover, it has undertaken

Figure 9.1  Tourist at Leopold's Café, Mumbai.

'a series of promotional initiatives to minimise the negative impact of the global economic meltdown and the terrorist attack in Mumbai and to promote tourism to India' (Ministry of Tourism, 2010: 64). These have included various 'roadshows' in developing markets such as Russia, Scandinavia, Australia and the Middle East, focusing, in particular, on showcasing adventure tourism, nature-based tourism, health tourism and sports tourism (emphasising New Delhi as the host of the 2010 Commonwealth Games), as well as India's cuisine, as niche tourism sectors (Ministry of Tourism, 2010). Moreover, the Ministry of Tourism also aims to get India's South-East Asian neighbours to visit India in greater numbers, for example by creating a special Buddhist circuit, distinguishing this Asian market from other international markets.

Nevertheless, India's tourism promotion and development is still rather fragmented geographically. Although some places are highly developed and promoted as distinct destinations, such as Goa, Rajasthan or Kerala, others still need to develop basic tourism infrastructure. In this context, recently the Ministry of Tourism revised the Market Development Assistance scheme to help motivate travel agents and tour operators to promote lesser-known destinations in India. The social dimensions of this policy initiative have sought to provide capacity building for rural tourism and sustainable livelihoods through community participation and empowerment, training and skills development (Ministry of Tourism, 2009a). These programmes may appear progressive considering the rather conservative social context in rural areas, where older traditional values define the caste, class and gender relationships.

However, it is not necessarily simply a matter of accommodation supply by the Indian Tourism Development Corporation, but sometimes more a question of mobility in terms of how to even reach a particular destination. Although huge progress has been made in recent years to improve travel connections within India, either by air or by land, there is still a long way to go. Nevertheless, before building roads for foreign tourists and adding more tourist trains for domestic middle class travellers a number of other development issues have to be recognised. In particular, when reflecting on international tourism to India there can be an impression that tourism does not so much help India's all-round development, but reinforces the discrepancies between the rich and the poor in the country. However, on the other hand, managed in a sensitive way, tourism may be an important source of economic development funding and also help with social development for particular communities in India. Hence, the politics of tourism development in India remain paramount.

## A research agenda for tourism and India

Throughout this book we have tried to emphasise the need for a critical approach to the study of the relations between tourism and India and it is our belief that much more critically orientated research needs to be carried out. We advocate a qualitative, ethnographic approach for this research in line with contemporary debates in the social sciences. Contemporary research into tourism has highlighted the need for further research into the embodied, performative nature of much tourist behaviour as well as the interactions of tourists with their hosts. Such research also needs to sensitive to the political and politicised nature of tourism development processes both within India and in relation to India in a global context of various mobilities that we discussed in Chapter 8. In this final section of the book we thus wish to list some aspects of tourism and India that we feel need particular attention from both managerial and experiential perspectives.

- *Accommodation* – India's hotel sector is rapidly developing and research needs to continue into this varied sector.
- *Adventure tourism* – This niche sector has been prioritised by the Indian government recently as an area for future development, particularly in mountainous regions.
- *Airports* – Further research is needed into the changing nature of both domestic and international aeromobility in India.
- *Climate change* – India as a destination is susceptible to many varied environmental problems and research into the potential impacts of climate change is thus crucial.
- *Community development* – As tourism in India expands, research will continue to be needed into local impacts of tourism and into how communities can benefit from tourism in a sustainable manner.
- *Crisis management* – As the recent terrorist attacks in Mumbai testify, India needs to be able to respond better to the impact that these threats have on the tourism industry.
- *Diaspora relations* – As we have noted in this book, India has begun to look to her diaspora recently as a source of both tourists as well as investment and this trend will need to be closely monitored.
- *Ecotourism* – It remains to be seen how India's national parks develop environmentally sensitive forms of tourism in the future in the face of biotic pressures.
- *Education* – Tourism as an area of study in India is still rather undeveloped and further research is needed into this sector in a global context of changing further and higher education initiatives.
- *Events and festivals* – India has some of the world's largest religious festivals and has more recently begun to host major international events.
- *Film tourism* – In this book we have dwelt quite significantly on the ways in which Bollywood, in particular, has exerted a great influence on contemporary tourism in India.
- *Gastronomy* – The gastro-politics of tourism in India is highly under-researched, although India has a unique take on food and drink.
- *Gender relations* – Contemporary tourism research has highlighted that tourism is emphatically a gendered enterprise and further research is needed into the complex gender and sexual relations that constitute tourism in India.
- *Health and medical tourism* – This book has highlighted the ways in which

health and medical tourism have been recently developed in India and this will continue to be an area of research.

- *Information and communication technology (ICT)* – India, as we have seen, has one of the largest uses of mobile phones, and as this technology develops we see the need to research the changing relations between ICT and tourism in the Indian context.
- *Mass tourism* – As India's middle classes expand, India will continue to experience further mass tourism development and this is still under-researched.
- *Sports tourism* – At the time of writing India is preparing to host the Commonwealth Games in New Delhi, and India has for a long period been a destination for cricket sports tourists, and this remains to be researched.
- *Themed attractions* – India has begun to develop new themed tourist attractions – including a new dinosaur theme park in Gujarat aimed primarily at middle-class domestic visitors – and these will need researching.
- *Transport* – Tourism always relies on transport, and, as we have highlighted at various points in this book, tourism in India frequently relies on the experiences of India's network of trains.

# References

AAI. 2010. *Welcome to AAI*. Available online: http://www.aai.aero/AAI/main.jsp

Abraham, R. 2007. Mobile phones and economic development: Evidence from the fishing industry in India. *Information Technologies and International Development* 4(1), 5–17.

Ahmed, S., Castaneda, C., Fortier, A. and Sheller, M. (eds). 2003. *Uprootings/Regroundings: Questions of home and migration*. Oxford: Berg.

Ahuja, O. P. 1999. Domestic tourism and its linkage with international tourism – Indian case study. In Bhardwaj, D. S., Chaudhary, M. and Kamra, K. K. (eds) *Domestic Tourism in India*. New Delhi: Indus Publishing Company.

Airault, R. 2002. *Fous d'Inde*. Paris: Payot.

Aitchison, C. 2001. Theorizing Other discourses of tourism, gender and culture: Can the subaltern speak (in tourism)? *Tourist Studies* 1(2), 133–147.

Aitken, E. 1897. *A Naturalist on the Prowl or in the Jungle*. Calcutta: Thacker.

de Alwis, R. 2010. Promoting tourism in South Asia. In Ahmed, S., Kelegama, S. and Ghani, E. (eds) *Promoting Economic Cooperation in South Asia*. Singapore: Sage.

Anderson, B. 1983. *Imagined Communities: Reflections on the origin and spread of nationalism*. London: Verso.

Appadurai, A. 1988. How to make a national cuisine: Cookbooks in contemporary India. *Comparative Studies in Society and History* 30(1), 3–24.

Appadurai, A. and Breckenridge, C. 1999. Museums are good to think: Heritage on view in India. In Boswell, D. and Evans, J. (eds) *Representing the Nation: A reader*. London: Routledge.

Appayya, M. 2001. *Management Plan for Rajiv Gandhi (Nagarahole) National Park (2000–2010)*. Mysore: Karnataka Forest Department.

Apunkachoice.com. 2007. *UK to Attract More Tourists to Bollywood Film Locations*. Available online: http://www.apunkachoice.com/happenings/20070528–0.html

Aramberri, J. 1991. *The Nature of Youth Tourism: Motivations, characteristics and requirements*. Paper presented at the 1991 International Conference on Youth Tourism, New Delhi. Madrid: World Tourism Organisation.

ASI (Archaeological Survey of India). 2004. *Archaeological Survey of India, Activities*. New Delhi: Ministry of Tourism and Culture. Available online: http://asi.nic.in/activities.html

ASI (Archaeological Survey of India) and CRCI (Cultural Resource Conservation Initiative). 2009. *Comprehensive Conservation Management Plan: The Red Fort*. Delhi: ASI.

Assam Tourism. 2010. *Welcome to Assam Tourism.* Available online: http://www. assamtourism.org/

Baedeker, K. 1887. *London and Its Environs.* Leipzig: Karl Baedeker.

Baerenholdt, J., Framke, W., Larsen, J. and Urry, J. 2004. *Performing Tourist Places.* London: Ashgate.

Bahadur Singh, I. 1979. *The Other India: The overseas Indians and their relationship with India.* New Delhi: Arnold-Heinemann.

Baker, K. 2009. *The Changing Tourist Gaze in India's Hill Stations: From the early nineteenth century to the present.* Environment, Politics and Development Working Paper Series. London: Department of Geography, King's College. Available online: http://www.kcl.ac.uk/schools/sspp/geography/research/epd/working.html

Ballabh, V., Balooni, K. and Dave, S. 2002. Why local resources management institutions decline: A comparative analysis of *van* (forest) *panchayats* and forest protection committees in India. *World Development* 30(12), 2153–2167.

Bandyopadhyay, R. 2008. Nostalgia, identity and tourism: Bollywood in the Indian diaspora. *Journal of Tourism and Cultural Change* 6(2), 79–100.

Bandyopadhyay, R. and Morais, D. 2005. Representative dissonance: India's self and western image. *Annals of Tourism Research* 32(4), 1006–1021.

Bandyopadhyay, R., Morais, D. and Chick, G. 2008. Religion and identity in India's heritage tourism. *Annals of Tourism Research* 35(3), 790–808.

Barber, B. J. 2001. *Jihad vs. McWorld: Terrorism's challenge to democracy.* New York: Ballantyne Books.

Baruah, S. 2001. *India against Itself: Assam and the politics of nationality.* New Delhi: Oxford University Press.

Basu, P. 2007. *Highland Homecomings: Genealogy and heritage-tourism in the Scottish diaspora.* London: Routledge.

Baudrillard, J. 1994. *Simulacra and Simulations.* Ann Arbor, MI: University of Michigan Press.

Bautès, N. 2006. *Le goût de l'héritage: Processus de production d'un territoire touristique: Udaipur en Inde du Nord (Rajasthan).* Thèse de doctorat présentée et soutenue publiquement par le 14 décembre 2004. Available online: http://tel.archives-ouvertes.fr/

BBC News. 2003a. Two die in Assam ethnic clashes. 23 November.

BBC News. 2003b. Over 17,000 flee Assam violence. 26 November.

BBC News. 2003c. Tea manager shot dead in Assam. 26 May.

BBC News. 2003d. Assam tea manager killed. 7 July.

BBC News. 2003e. Assam on alert after rebel threat. 14 November.

BBC News. 2003f. Army to guard Assam tea estate. 13 October.

BBC News. 2003g. Indian PM firm on Assam violence. 20 November.

BBC News. 2004. Screws tighten on Indian rebels. 2 January.

Beeton, S. 2005. *Film-Induced Tourism.* Clevedon: Channel View.

Bennett, T. 1995. *The Birth of the Museum.* London: Routledge.

Berger, A. A. 2008. *The Golden Triangle: An ethnic-semiotic tour of present-day India.* New Brunswick: Transaction Publishers.

Best, J. W. 1931. *Indian Shikar Notes.* 3rd edn. Lahore: Pioneer.

Beteille, A. 2001. The Indian middle classes. *Times of India*, 5 February.

Beteille, A. 2006. *Ideology and Social Science.* New Delhi: Penguin.

Bhabha, H. 1994. *The Location of Culture.* London: Routledge.

Bhachu, P. 1999. Multiple-migrants and multiple diasporas: Cultural reproduction and transformations among British Punjabi women. In C. Petievich (ed.) *The Expanding Landscape: South Asians and the diaspora*. New Delhi: Manohar.

Bhardwaj, S. 1973. *Hindu Places of Pilgrimage in India*. Berkeley: University of California Press.

Bhardwaj, S. and Madhusudana Rao, N. 1990. Asian Indians in the United States: A geographic appraisal. In Clarke, C., Peach, C. and Vertovec, S. (eds) *South Asians Overseas: Migration and ethnicity*. Cambridge: Cambridge University Press.

Bhattacharya, N. 1986. Colonial state and agrarian society. In Bhattacharya, S. and Thapar, R. (eds) *Situating Indian History*. Delhi: Oxford University Press.

Bhattacharya, P. 2001. Tourism. In Bhagabati, A., Bora, A. and Kar, B. (eds) *Geography of Assam*. New Delhi: Rajesh.

Bhaumik, S. 2008. Fears over Assam vigilante violence. *BBC News*, 8 September.

Bhaumik, S. 2010. Remote state in vanguard of Indian mobile phone craze. *BBC News*, 23 April. Available online: http://news.bbc.co.uk/1/hi/8640473.stm

Bies, W. and Zacharia, L. 2007. Medical tourism: Outsourcing surgery. *Mathematical and Computer Modelling* 46, 1144–1159.

Blaikie, P. and Brookfield, H. 1987. *Land Degradation and Society*. London: Methuen.

Blunt, A. 2005. *Domicile and Diaspora: Anglo-Indian women and the spatial politics of home*. Oxford: Wiley-Blackwell.

Bonney, R. 2003. Introduction. In Hartung, J., Hawkes, G. and Bhattacharjee, A. (eds) *Ayodhya 1992–2003: The assertion of cultural and religious hegemony*. Leicester: University of Leicester, Centre for the History of Religious and Political Pluralism.

Bookman, M. Z. and Bookman, K. R. 2007. *Medical Tourism in Developing Countries*. New York: Palgrave Macmillan.

Bostock, S. 1993. *Zoos and Animal Rights: The ethics of keeping animals*. London: Routledge.

Bradt, H. 1995. Better to travel cheaply? *The Independent on Sunday*, 12 February, p. 49.

Brah, A. 1996. *Cartographies of Diaspora: Contesting identities*. London: Routledge.

Brayton, S. 2007. MTV's jackass: Transgression, abjection and the economy of white masculinity. *Journal of Gender Studies* 16(1), 57–72.

Brockmann, T. 2002. Bollywood singt und tanzt in der Schweiz. In Schneider, A. (ed.) *Das Indische Kino und die Schweiz*. Zürich: Edition Museum für Gestaltung S.

Brown, J. M. 1887. *Shikar Sketches with Notes on Indian Field-Sports*. London: Hurst.

Bryant, R. 1992. Political ecology: An emerging research agenda in Third-World studies. *Political Geography* 11(1), 12–36.

Bryant, R. and Bailey, S. 1997. *Third World Political Ecology*. London: Routledge.

Buckley, R. 2004. The effects of world heritage listing on tourism to Australian national parks. *Journal of Sustainable Tourism* 12(1), 70–84.

Butler, R. 1990. The concept of the tourist area cycle of evolution: Implications for the management of resources. *The Canadian Geographer* 24(11), 5–12.

Campbell, G. and Hughes, J. 1995. Plague in India: A new warning from an old nemesis. *Annals of Internal Medicine* 122(2), 151–153.

Capella-Cervera, J.-E. and Priestley, G. 2008. Determinants of the spatial pattern of cultural tours: A case study of Spanish package tourists in India. In Jansen-Verbeke, M., Priestley, G. and Russo, P. (eds) *Cultural Resources for Tourism*. New York: Novascience.

Catibog-Sinha, C. 2008. Zoo tourism: Biodiversity conservation through tourism. *Journal of Ecotourism* 7(2), 160–178.

Chand, M. 1998. Domestic tourism in Himachal Pradesh: Potential, policies and trends. In

Bhardwaj, D. S., Chaudhary, M. and Kamra, K. K. (eds) *Domestic Tourism in India.* New Delhi: Indus Publishing.

Chandra, B. 1991. The strategy of the Indian National Congress. In Hill, J. (ed.) *The Congress and Indian Nationalism: Historical perspectives.* London: Curzon Press.

Chang, T. C. 1999. Local uniqueness in the global village: Heritage tourism in Singapore. *Professional Geographer* 51(1), 91–103.

Chatterjee, P. 2001. *A Time for Tea: Women, labor and post/colonial politics on an Indian plantation.* Durham, NC: Duke University Press.

Chaudhary, M. 1996. India's tourism: A paradoxical product. *Tourism Management* 17(8), 616–619.

Chaudhary, M. 2000. India's image as a tourist destination – a perspective of foreign tourists. *Tourism Management* 21, 293–297.

Cheong, S.-M. and Miller, M. 2000. Power and tourism: A Foucauldian observation. *Annals of Tourism Research* 29(2), 371–390.

Church, A. and Coles, T. 2007. Tourism and the many faces of power. In Church, A. and Coles, T. (eds) *Tourism, Power and Space.* London: Routledge.

Churchman, D. 1985. The educational impact of zoos and museums: A review of the literature. *Resources in Education* 20(12), 133–161.

Clark, G. and Dear, M. 1984. *State Apparatus: Structures of language and legitimacy.* Boston: Allen and Unwin.

Clarke, C., Peach, C. and Vertovec, S. (eds). 1990. *South Asians Overseas: Migration and ethnicity.* Cambridge: Cambridge University Press.

Cohen, E. 1972. Towards a sociology of international tourism. *Social Research* 39(1), 164–182.

Cohen, E. 1973. Nomads from affluence: Notes on the phenomenon of drifter-tourism. *International Journal of Comparative Sociology* 14(1), 89–103.

Cohen, E. 1992. Pilgrimage centers, concentric and excentric. *Annals of Tourism Research* 19(1), 33–50.

Cohen, R. 1997. *Global Diasporas: An introduction.* London: UCL Press.

Cohen, R. 2008. The effects of WHS designation on potential visitors to heritage sites. MBA thesis, The Guilford Glazer Faculty of Business and Management, Ben Gurion University of the Negev, Israel.

Cohen, S. 2010. Re-conceptualising lifestyle travellers: Contemporary 'drifters'. In Hannam, K. and Diekmann, A. (eds) *Beyond Backpacker Tourism: Mobilities and experiences.* Clevedon: Channel View.

Cohn, B. 1983. Representing authority in Victorian India. In Hobsbawm, E. and Ranger, T. (eds) *The Invention of Tradition.* Cambridge: Cambridge University Press.

Cohn, B. 1987. The recruitment and training of British civil servants in India, 1600–1860. In Cohn, B. (ed.) *An Anthropologist among the Historians and Other Essays.* New Delhi: Oxford University Press.

Coles, T. and Timothy, D. (eds). 2004. *Tourism, Diasporas and Space.* London: Routledge.

Conforti, J. M. 1996. Ghettos as tourism attractions. *Annals of Tourism Research* 23(4), 830–842.

Connell, J. 2006. Medical tourism: Sea, sun, sand and surgery. *Tourism Management* 27, 1093–1100.

Cook, S. 1993. *Imperial Affinities: Nineteenth century analogies and exchanges between India and Ireland.* New Delhi: Sage.

Corbett, J. 1944. *Man-Eaters of Kumaon.* Oxford: Oxford University Press.

Corbridge, S. and Simpson, E. 2006. Militant cartographies and traumatic spaces: Ayodhya,

Bhuj and the contested geographies of Hindutva. In Raju, S., Kumar, S. and Corbridge, S. (eds) *Colonial and Post-colonial Geographies of India.* New Delhi: Sage.

Costa, R. M. 2009. Take a 10-day tour of India for just Rs 5K. *The Times of India*, 29 January, p. 4.

Crosby, A. 2004. *Ecological Imperialism: The biological expansion of Europe, 900–1900.* Cambridge: Cambridge University Press.

CZA. 2009. *Central Zoo Authority of India – About Us.* Available online: http://www.cza. nic.in/

Dalrymple, W. 1993. *City of Djinns.* London: HarperCollins.

Dalrymple, W. 1998. *The Age of Kali: Indian travels and encounters.* London: HarperCollins.

Dalrymple, W. 2003. Porous boundaries and cultural crossover: Fanny Parkes and 'going native'. In Mohanty, S. (ed.) *Travel Writing and the Empire*. New Delhi: Katha.

Dalrymple, W. 2007. Preface. In Fisher, M. (ed.) *Visions of Mughal India: An anthology of European travel writing.* London: I. B. Tauris.

D'Andrea, A. 2006. Neo-nomadism: A theory of post-identitarian mobility in the global age. *Mobilities* 1(1), 95–119.

Dann, G. 1999. Theoretical issues for tourism's future development. In Pearce, D. and Butler, R. (eds) *Contemporary Issues in Tourism Development.* London: Routledge.

Datta, P. 2009. For us, Ambedkar is father of the nation. *The Times of India*, 12 July. Available online: http://timesofindia.indiatimes.com/Mumbai/For-us-Ambedkar-i s-father-of-the-nation-/articleshow/4767615.cms

Delhimonuments.info. 2009. *India Gate (All-India War Memorial).* Available online: http://www.delhimonuments.info/india-gate.html

Department of Tourism, Kerala. 2002. *Tourism Vision 2025*. Available online: http://www. kerala.gov.in/keralacallingoct/tourism2.pdf

Department of Tourism, Kerala. 2010. *Tourism Statistics*. Available online: http://www. keralatourism.org/touriststatistics.php

Desmond, J. 1999. *Staging Tourism: Bodies on display from Waikiki to Sea World.* Chicago: University of Chicago Press.

Dhariwal, R. 2005. Tourist arrivals in India: How important are domestic disorders. *Tourism Economics* 11(2), 185–205.

Diekmann, A. and Maulet, G. 2009. A contested ethnic tourism asset: The case of Matonge in Brussels. *Tourism, Culture and Communication* 9(1), 93–106.

Diekmann, A. and Maulet, G. 2010. Diversifying the tourism product in Brussels. In Maitland, R. and Ritchie, B. W. (eds) *National Capital Tourism: Marketing, development and planning issues.* Wallingford: CABI.

Di Giovine, M. A. 2009. *The Heritage-scape: UNESCO, world heritage and tourism.* Plymouth: Lexington Books.

DNA India. 2009. *Animal Rights Groups Seek Closure of Mumbai Zoo.* Available online: http://www.dnaindia.com/mumbai/report_animal-rights-groups-see k-closure-of-mumbai-zoo_1252499

Douglas, M. 1966. *Purity and Danger.* London: Routledge.

Dreze, J. and Sen, A. 1995. *India, Economic Development and Social Opportunity.* Oxford: Oxford University Press.

Dubey, D. 2001. *Kumbha Mela: Pilgrimage to the greatest cosmic fair.* Allahabad: Society of Pilgrimage Studies.

Dunlop, R. H. W. 1860. *Hunting in the Himalaya.* London: Bentley.

Duval, D. 2003. When hosts become guests: Return visits and diasporic identities in a

Commonwealth Eastern Caribbean community. *Current Issues in Tourism* 6(4), 267–308.

Dwyer, R. 2001. The Indian middle classes, romance and consumerism. In Schneider, A. (ed.) *Bollywood in Switzerland*. New Delhi: The British Council.

Dwyer, R. and Patel, D. 2002. *Cinema India: The visual culture of Hindi film*. London: Reaktion.

Eade, J. 2000. Introduction to the Illinois paperback. In Eade, J. And Sallnow, M. (eds) *Contesting the Sacred: The anthropology of Christian pilgrimage*. Chicago: University of Illinois Press.

Eagles, P. and McCool, S. 2002. *Tourism in National Parks and Protected Areas: Planning and management*. Wallingford: CABI.

Edensor, T. 1998. *Tourists at the Taj*. London: Routledge.

Edensor, T. 2001. Performing tourism, staging tourism: (Re)producing tourist space and practice. *Tourist Studies* 1(1), 59–81.

Edensor, T. 2002. *National Identity, Popular Culture and Everyday Life*. Oxford: Berg.

Edensor, T. 2004. Reconstituting the Taj Mahal: tourist flows and glocalization. In Sheller, M. and Urry, J. (eds) *Tourism Mobilities: Places to play, places in play*. London: Routledge.

Epelde, K. 2004. Travel guidebooks to India: a century and a half of orientalism. PhD thesis, English Studies Program, University of Wollongong. Available online: http://ro.uow.edu.au/theses/195

Featherstone, M. 1995. *Undoing Culture: Globalization, postmodernism and identity*. London: Sage.

Feldhaus, A. 2003. *Connected Places: Religion, pilgrimage and geographical imagination in India*. New York: Palgrave.

Fernandes, L. 2007. *India's New Middle Class: Democratic politics in an era of economic reform*. Minneapolis: University of Minnesota Press.

Finch, J. 2007. Indian tourists worth more to London than Japanese. *Guardian*, 7 May.

Fisher, M. 2007. Introduction. In Fisher, M. (ed.) *Visions of Mughal India: An anthology of European travel writing*. London: I. B. Tauris.

Fonia, R. 2002. *1857 Memorial Museum, Residency, Lucknow*. Lucknow: Archaeological Survey of India.

Fortier, A. M. 2000. *Migrant Belongings: Memory, space, identity*. Oxford: Berg.

Fowler, S. 2003. Ancestral tourism. *Insights*, March: D31–D36.

Freire-Meideros, M. 2009. The favela and its touristic transits. *Geoforum* 40, 580–588.

Friedmann, J. 1999. The hybridization of roots and the abhorrence of the bush. In Featherstone, M. and Lash, S. (eds) *Spaces of Culture*. London: Sage.

Frykenberg, R. (ed.). 1979. *Land Control and Social Structure in Indian History*. New Delhi: Manohar.

Gadgil, M. and Guha, R. 1995. *Ecology and Equity*. London: Routledge.

George, B. 2009. Medical tourism in India: A case study of Apollo Hospitals. In Smith, M. and Puczko, L. (eds) *Health and Wellness Tourism*. Oxford: Butterworth-Heinemann.

Ghosh, A. 2003. The diaspora in Indian culture. In Chandrasekhar, I. and Seel, P. (eds) *Body.City: Siting contemporary culture in India*. New Delhi: Tulika Books.

Gilroy, P. 1993. *The Black Atlantic: Modernity and double consciousness*. London: Verso.

Gladstone, D. L. 2005. *From Pilgrimage to Package Tour: Travel and tourism in the Third World*. New York: Routledge.

Gladstone, D. and Fainstein, S. 2001. Tourism in US global cities: A comparison of New York and Los Angeles. *Journal of Urban Affairs* 23(1), 23–40.

Glasfurd, A. 1928. *Musings of an Old Shikari: Reflections on life and sport in jungle India.* London: John Lane.

Gogia, N. 2006. Unpacking corporeal mobilities: The global voyages of labour and leisure. *Environment and Planning A* 38, 359–375.

Goodwin, H. 1999. Backpackers good, package tourists bad? *In Focus* 31, 12–13.

Goodwin, H. 2000. Tourism, national parks and partnerships. In Butler, R. and Boyd, S. (eds) *Tourism and National Parks.* Chichester: Wiley.

Goodwin, H. 2002. Local community involvement in tourism around national parks: Opportunities and constraints. *Current Issues in Tourism* 5(3), 338–360.

Gordon, B. 1986. The souvenir: Messenger of the extraordinary. *Journal of Popular Culture* 20(3), 135–146.

Gossling, S. (ed.). 2003. *Tourism and Development in Tropical Islands: Political ecology perspectives.* London: Edward Elgar.

Graburn, N. 2001. Relocating the tourist. *International Sociology* 16(2), 147–158.

Graham, A. 2008. *Managing Airports: An international perspective.* Oxford: Butterworth-Heinemann.

Graham, B., Ashworth, G. and Tunbridge, J. 2000. *A Geography of Heritage.* London: Arnold.

Grove, R. 1996. *Green Imperialism: Colonial expansion, tropical island Edens and the origins of environmentalism.* Cambridge: Cambridge University Press.

Gupta, V. 1999. Sustainable tourism: Learning from Indian religious traditions. *International Journal of Contemporary Hospitality Management* 11(2/3), 91–95.

Hall, C. M. 1994. *Tourism and Politics: Policy, power and place.* London: Wiley.

Hall, C. M. and Jenkins, J. 1995. *Tourism and Public Policy.* London: Thomson.

Hall, C. M. and Page, S. (eds). 2000. *Tourism in South and South East Asia: Issues and cases.* Oxford: Butterworth Heinemann.

Hall, C. M. and Piggin, R. 2001. Tourism and world heritage in OECD countries. *Tourism Recreation Research* 26, 103–105.

Hall, C. M. and Tucker, H. 2004. *Tourism and Postcolonialism: Contested discourses, identities and representations.* London: Routledge.

Hampton, M. P. 1998. Backpacker tourism and economic development. *Annals of Tourism Research* 25(3), 639–660.

Hampton, M. P. 2005. Heritage, local communities and economic development. *Annals of Tourism Research* 32(3), 735–759

Hannam, K. 1998. The Indian Forest Service: A cultural geography. PhD thesis, University of Portsmouth, Portsmouth.

Hannam, K. 1999. Environmental management in India. *Journal of Environmental Planning and Management* 42(2), 221–233.

Hannam, K. 2004a. Tourism and forest management in India: The role of the state in limiting tourism development. *Tourism Geographies* 6(3), 331–351.

Hannam, K. 2004b. Tourism and development II: Marketing destinations, experiences and crises. *Progress in Development Studies* 4(3), 256–263.

Hannam, K. 2004c. The ambivalences of diaspora tourism in India. In Coles, T. and Timothy, D. (eds) *Tourism, Diaspora and Space.* London: Routledge.

Hannam, K. 2005a. Tea, tourism and the search for independence in Assam: A political ecology. In Jolliffe, L. (ed.) *Tea and Tourism: Tourists, traditions and transformations.* Clevedon: Channel View.

Hannam, K. 2005b. Tourism management issues in India's national parks: An analysis of the Rajiv Gandhi (Nagarahole) National Park. *Current Issues in Tourism* 8(2), 165–180.

Hannam, K. 2006. Contested discourses of war and heritage at the British Residency, Lucknow, India. *International Journal of Tourism Research* 8(3), 199–212.

Hannam, K. 2008. The end of tourism? Nomadology and the mobilities paradigm. In Tribe, J. (ed.) *Philosophical Issues in Tourism*. Clevedon: Channel View.

Hannam, K. 2009. Ayurvedic health tourism in Kerala, India. In Smith, M. and Puczko, L. (eds) *Health and Wellness Tourism*. Oxford: Butterworth-Heinemann.

Hannam, K. 2011. Heterogeneous spaces of tourism and recreation at Mumbai Zoo, India. In Frost, W. (ed.) *Zoos and Tourism*. Clevedon: Channel View.

Hannam, K. and Ateljevic, I. (eds). 2008. *Backpacker Tourism: Concepts and profiles*. Clevedon: Channel View.

Hannam, K. and Diekmann, A. (eds). 2010. *Beyond Backpacker Tourism: Mobilities and experiences*. Clevedon: Channel View.

Hannam, K. and Knox, D. 2010. *Understanding Tourism: A critical introduction*. London: Sage.

Hannam, K., Sheller, M. and Urry, J. 2006. Editorial: Mobilities, immobilities and moorings. *Mobilities* 1(1), 1–22.

Hardgrove, A. 2007. Shifting terrains of heritage: The painted towns of Shekhawati. In Henderson, C. and Weisgrau, M. (eds) *Raj Rhapsodies: Tourism, heritage and the seduction of history*. Aldershot: Ashgate.

Hazarika, I. 2009. Medical tourism: Its potential impact on the health workforce and health systems in India. *Health Policy and Planning* 25(3), 248–251.

Henderson, C. and Weisgrau, M. (eds). 2007. *Raj Rhapsodies: Tourism, heritage and the seduction of history*. Aldershot: Ashgate.

Hewison, R. 1987. *The Heritage Industry*. London: Methuen.

Hollinshead, K. 1998. Tourism, hybridity and ambiguity: The relevance of Bhabha's 'Third Space' cultures. *Journal of Leisure Research* 30(1), 121–156.

Hollinshead, K. 1999. Surveillance of the worlds of tourism: Foucault and the eye-of-power. *Tourism Management* 20, 7–23.

Hollinshead, K. 2004. Tourism and new sense: Worldmaking and the enunciative value of tourism. In Hall, C. M. and Tucker, H. (eds) *Tourism and Postcolonialism: Contested discourse, identities and representations*. London: Routledge.

Hottola, P. 1999. *The Intercultural Body: Western woman, culture confusion and control of space in the South Asian travel scene*. Publications of the Department of Geography, No. 7. Joensuu: University of Joensuu.

Hottola, P. 2002. Touristic encounters with the exotic West: Blondes on the screens and streets of India. *Tourism Recreation Research* 27(1), 83–89.

Hottola, P. 2004. Culture confusion: Intercultural adaptation in tourism. *Annals of Tourism Research* 31(2), 447–466.

Hottola, P. 2005. The metaspatialities of control management in tourism: Backpacking in India. *Tourism Geographies* 7(1), 1–22.

Hudson, S. and Ritchie, J. R. B. 2006. Promoting destinations via film tourism: An empirical identification of supporting marketing initiatives. *Journal of Travel Research* 44(4), 387–396.

Hunter-Jones, P. and Hayward, C. 1998. Leisure consumption and the United Kingdom zoo. In Ravenscroft, N., Philips, D. and Bennett, M. (eds) *Leisure, Culture and Commerce*. Brighton: LSA.

Hutnyk, J. 1996. *The Rumour of Calcutta: Tourism, charity and the poverty of representation*. London: Zed.

Inden, R. 1995. Embodying God: From imperial progresses to national progress in India. *Economy and Society* 24(2), 245–278.

Irwin, R. 2007. Culture shock: Negotiating feelings in the field. *Anthropology Matters* 9(1), 1–11.

ITOPC. 2010. *Indian Tour Operators Promotion Council*. Available online: http://www.itopc.org/travel-requisite/tourism-statistics.html

Ivanovic, M. 2009. *Cultural Tourism*. Landsdowne: Juta Academic.

Jansen-Verbeke, M. 1986. Inner-city tourism: Resources, tourists and promoters. *Annals of Tourism Research* 13, 79–100.

Jarvis, J. and Peel, V. 2010. Flashpacking in Fiji: Reframing the 'global nomad' in a developing destination. In Hannam, K. and Diekmann, A. (eds) *Beyond Backpacker Tourism: Mobilities and experiences*. Clevedon: Channel View.

Jewitt, S. 1995. Europe's 'Other'? Forestry policy and practices in colonial and postcolonial India. *Society and Space* 13(1), 67–90.

Jhala, J. 2007. From privy purse to global purse: Maharaja Gaj Singh's role in the marketing of heritage and philanthropy. In Henderson, C. and Weisgrau, M. (eds) *Raj Rhapsodies: Tourism, heritage and the seduction of history*. Aldershot: Ashgate.

Johnson, N. 1999. Framing the past: Time, space and the politics of heritage tourism in Ireland. *Political Geography* 18, 187–207.

Joseph, M. 1999. *Nomadic Identities: The performance of citizenship*. Minneapolis, MN: University of Minnesota Press.

Joseph, C. and Kavoori, A. 2001. Mediated resistance: Tourism and the host community. *Annals of Tourism Research* 28(4), 998–1009.

Joshi, S. and Pant, P. 1990. Environmental implications of the recent growth of tourism in Nainital, Kumaun Himalaya, UP, India. *Mountain Research and Development* 10, 347–357.

Jutla, R. 2000. Visual image of the city: tourists' versus residents' perception of Simla, a hill station in northern India. *Tourism Geographies* 2(4), 404–420.

Jutla, R. 2006. Pilgrimage in the Sikh tradition. In Timothy, D. J. and Olsen, D. H. (eds) *Tourism, Religion, and Spiritual Journeys*. London: Routledge.

Kakar, S. 2007. *Indian Identity*. New Delhi: Penguin Books India.

Kant, A. 2009. *Branding India: An incredible story*. New Delhi: Harper Collins.

Kennedy, D. 1996. *The Magic Mountains: Hill stations and the British Raj*. Berkeley: University of California Press.

Kerr, W. 2003. *Tourism, Public Policy and the Strategic Management of Failure*. London: Pergamon.

Khan, M. S. 1998. Domestic tourism in India. In Bhardwaj, D. S., Chaudhary, M. and Kamra, K. K. (eds) *Domestic Tourism in India*. New Delhi: Indus Publishing Company.

Khanna, R. 2009. *IRCTC's Bharat Darshan from west, south zones too*. Available online: http://www.financialexpress.com/news/irctcsbharatdarshanfromwest-southzonestoo/410381/

Kothari, A., Suri, S. and Singh, N. 1995. People and protected areas: Rethinking conservation in India. *The Ecologist* 25(5), 88–194.

Koven, S. 2004. *Slumming: Sexual and social politics in Victorian London*. Princeton: Princeton University Press.

Kristeva, J. 1982. *Powers of Horror: An essay on abjection*. New York: Columbia University Press.

Kumar, S. 2002. Does 'participation' in common pool resource management help the poor?

A social cost–benefit analysis of Joint Forest Management in Jharkhand, India. *World Development* 30(5), 763–782.

Lall, M. C. 2001. *India's Missed Opportunity: India's relationship with the non resident Indians*. Aldershot: Ashgate.

Leonard, K. 1999. Construction of identity in diaspora: Emigrants from Hyderabad, India. In Petievich, C. (ed.) *The Expanding Landscape: South Asians and the diaspora*. New Delhi: Manohar.

Lessinger, J. 1999. Class, race and success: Indian-Americans confront the American Dream. In Petievich, C. (ed.) *The Expanding Landscape: South Asians and the diaspora*. New Delhi: Manohar.

Lin, J. 1995. Ethnic places, postmodernism, and urban change in Houston. *Sociological Quarterly* 36(4), 629–647.

Littrell, M., Anderson, L. and Brown, P. 1993. What makes a craft souvenir authentic? *Annals of Tourism Research* 20(1), 197–215.

Lowe, L. 1991. Heterogeneity, hybridity, multiplicity: Marking Asian American differences. *Diaspora* 1(1), 24–44.

MacCannell, D. 1973. Staged authenticity: Arrangements of social space in tourist settings. *American Journal of Sociology* 79, 589–603.

MacCannell, D. 1992. *Empty Meeting Grounds: The tourist papers*. London: Routledge.

MacDonald, S. 2003. *Holy Cow! An Indian adventure*. London: Bantam.

MacKenzie, J. 1988. *The Empire of Nature: Hunting, conservation and British imperialism*. Manchester: Manchester University Press.

McKercher, B. and Du Cros, H. 2002. *Cultural Tourism: The partnership between tourism and cultural heritage management*. New York: Haworth.

McKibben, B. 2009. *Kerala, India*. Available online: http://www.nationalgeographic.com/traveler/articles/1028kerala.html

MacLean, R. 2006. *Magic Bus: On the hippie trail from Istanbul to India*. London: Viking.

Magherini, G. 1992. *Syndrome di Stendhal*. Milan: Fettrinelli.

Mahajan, J. 1996. *The Grand Indian Tour: Travels and sketches of Emily Eden*. New Delhi: Manohar.

Maikhuri, R., Nautiyal, S., Rao, K. and Saxena, K. 2001. Conservation policy–people conflicts: A case study from Nanda Devi Biosphere Reserve (a World Heritage Site), India. *Forest Policy and Economics* 2, 355–365.

Maitland, R. 2007. Cultural tourism and the development of new tourism areas in London. In Richards, G. (ed.) *Cultural Tourism: Global and local perspectives*. London: Routledge.

Malbon, B. 1999. *Clubbing: Dancing, ecstasy and vitality*. London: Routledge.

Mandal, D. 2003. *Ayodhya, Archaeology after Demolition*. New Delhi: Orient Longman.

Mangan J. and Walvin, J. (eds). 1987. *Manliness and Morality: Middle class masculinity in Britain and America 1800–1940*. Manchester: Manchester University Press.

Mankekar, P. 2005. 'India shopping': Indian grocery stores and transnational configurations of belonging. In Watson, J. and Caldwell, M. (eds) *The Cultural Politics of Food and Eating: A reader*. Oxford: Blackwell.

Maoz, D. 2002. *India Will Love Me*. Jerusalem: Keter (in Hebrew).

Maoz, D. 2006. The mutual gaze. *Annals of Tourism Research* 33(1), 221–239.

Maoz, D. 2007. Backpackers' motivations: The role of culture and nationality. *Annals of Tourism Research* 34(1), 122–140.

Maoz, D. 2008. The backpacking journey of Israeli women in mid-life. In Hannam, K.

and Ateljevic, I. (eds) *Backpacker Tourism: Concepts and profiles.* Clevedon: Channel View.

Maoz, D. and Bekerman, Z. 2010. Searching for Jewish answers in Indian resorts: The postmodern traveler. *Annals of Tourism Research* 37(2), 423–439.

Mason, P. 2000. Zoo tourism: The need for more research. *Journal of Sustainable Tourism* 8(4), 333–339.

Mason, P. 2002. *Visitor Management in Protected Areas: Impacts or experiences.* Paper presented at the Tourism and the Natural Environment International Conference, University of Brighton, October.

Mathy, M. 2010. Usages touristiques de sites de Patrimoine Mondial de l'Unesco en Inde: Etude de cas: Sites du Red Fort et de Humayon's Tomb à Delhi. Master's dissertation in Tourism, Université Libre de Bruxelles, Brussels, Belgium.

Mawdsley, E. 2004. India's middle classes and the environment. *Development and Change* 35(1), 79–103.

Mawdsley, E., Mehra, D. and Beazley, K. 2009. Nature lovers, picnickers and bourgeois environmentalism. *Economic & Political Weekly*, 14 March, 49–59.

Menon, K. G. 2003. *The Residency, Lucknow.* New Delhi: Archaeological Survey of India.

Menon, S. 2003. Constitutive contradictions: Travel writing and construction of native women in colonial India. In Mohanty, S. (ed.) *Travel Writing and the Empire.* New Delhi: Katha.

Meethan, K. 2004. 'In the shoes of my ancestors': Tourism and genealogy. In Coles, T. and Timothy, D. (eds.) *Tourism, Diaspora and Space.* London: Routledge.

Mills, S. 1991. *Discourses of Difference: An analysis of women's travel writing and colonialism.* London: Routledge.

Ministry of Environment and Forests. 2003. *Annual Report.* New Delhi: Government of India.

Ministry of External Affairs. 2001. *The Indian Diaspora: Report of the High Level Committee on the Indian Diaspora.* New Delhi: Government of India.

Ministry of Tourism. 1999. *Annual Report.* New Delhi: Ministry of Tourism.

Ministry of Tourism. 2000. *Annual Report.* New Delhi: Government of India.

Ministry of Tourism. 2002. *National Tourism Policy.* New Delhi: Ministry of Tourism.

Ministry of Tourism. 2003. *Domestic Tourism Survey.* New Delhi: NCAER.

Ministry of Tourism. 2009a. Incredible India: Tourism statistics at a glance 2008. New Delhi: Ministry of Tourism.

Ministry of Tourism. 2009b. Guidelines for the scheme of Market development assistance for promotion of domestic tourism. With effect from the 09.01.2009. New Delhi: Ministry of Tourism.

Ministry of Tourism, 2010. *Annual Report.* New Delhi: Ministry of Tourism.

Ministry of Tourism and Culture. 2002. *Annual Report.* New Delhi: Government of India.

Mitra, A. 1999. *India through the Western Lens: Creating national images in film.* New Delhi: Sage.

Mohanty, S. 2003. Introduction: Beyond the imperial eye. In Mohanty, S. (ed.) *Travel Writing and the Empire.* New Delhi: Katha.

Morgan, N. and Pritchard, A. 2002. Contextualising destination branding. In Morgan, N., Pritchard, A. and Pride, R. (eds) *Destination Branding: Creating the unique destination proposition.* Oxford: Butterworth-Heinemann.

Morgan, N., Pritchard, A. and Pride, R. (eds). 2002. *Destination Branding: Creating the unique destination proposition.* Oxford: Butterworth-Heinemann.

Mowforth, M. and Munt, I. 1998. *Tourism and Sustainability: New tourism in the Third World.* London: Routledge.

Mullan, B. and Marvin, G. 1987. *Zoo Culture.* London: Weidenfeld and Nicolson.

Mumford, D. B. 1998. The measurement of culture shock. *Social Psychiatry and Epidemiology* 33, 149–154.

Municipal Corporation of Greater Mumbai. 2010. *Mumbai Human Development Report, 2009.* New Delhi: Oxford University Press.

Nanda, M. 2004. *Prophets Facing Backward: Postmodern critiques of science and Hindu nationalism.* London: Rutgers University Press.

Nash, C. 2000. Performativity in practice: Some recent work in cultural geography. *Progress in Human Geography* 24, 653–664.

Nash, C. 2002. Genealogical identities. *Environment and Planning D, Society and Space* 20, 27–52.

National Productivity Council. 2002. *Survey of Foreign Tourist's Expenses on Handicrafts.* New Delhi: Ministry of Tourism.

Nayar, M. 2009. Come Hither! India gets innovative to lure backpackers in times of crisis. *The Week*, 11 January, pp. 28–29.

Nayar, P. (ed.). 2009. *Days of the Raj: Life and leisure in British India.* New Delhi: Penguin.

Nyers, P. 2003. Abject cosmopolitanism: The politics of protection in the anti-deportation movement. *Third World Quarterly* 24(6), 1069–1093.

Oberg, K. 1960. Culture shock: Adjustment to new cultural environments. *Practical Anthropology* 7, 177–182.

Ong, A. 1999. *Flexible Citizenship: The cultural logics of transnationality.* Durham, NC: Duke University Press.

O'Reilly, K. 2000. *The British on the Costa del Sol: Transnational identities and local communities.* London: Routledge.

Palin, M. 1989. *Around the World in 80 Days.* London: BBC Books.

Palmer, C. 2005. An ethnography of Englishness: Experiencing identity through tourism. *Annals of Tourism Research* 32(1), 7–27.

Panagariya, A. 2008. *India: The emerging giant.* Oxford: Oxford University Press.

Pandian, A. S. 2001. Predatory care: The imperial hunt in Mughal and British India. *Journal of Historical Sociology* 14(1), 79–107.

Paris, C. 2010. The virtualization of backpacker culture: Virtual mooring, sustained interactions and enhanced mobilities. In Hannam, K. and Diekmann, A. (eds) *Beyond Backpacker Tourism: Mobilities and experiences.* Clevedon: Channel View.

Park, H. Y. 2010. Heritage tourism: Emotional journeys into nationhood. *Annals of Tourism Research* 37(1), 116–135.

Pedersen, J. 2000. Explaining economic liberalization in India: State and society perspectives. *World Development* 28(2), 265–282.

Peet, R. and Watts, M. (eds). 1996. *Liberation Ecologies: Environment, development, social movements.* London: Routledge.

Peluso, N. and Watts, M. 2001. *Violent Environments.* Ithaca, NY: Cornell University Press.

Phillips, R. 1997. *Mapping Men and Empire: A geography of adventure.* London: Routledge.

Pinney, C. 2001. Introduction: Public, popular and other cultures. In Dwyer, R. and Pinney, C. (eds) *Pleasure and the Nation: The history, politics and consumption of public culture in India.* Oxford: Oxford University Press.

Porter, L. 2007. Monaco targets Indian tourists. Available online: http://www.monaco-iq.com/monaco-targets-indian-tourists

Pratt, M. L. 1992. *Imperial Eyes: Travel writing and transculturalation*. London: Routledge.

Pretes, M. 2003. Tourism and nationalism. *Annals of Tourism Research* 30(1), 125–142.

Raguraman, K. 1998. Troubled passage to India. *Tourism Management* 19(6), 533–534.

Ramesh, R. 2007. Protests force India war grave visitors to end tour. *Guardian*, 27 September.

Rangarajan, M. 1996. *Fencing the Forest: Conservation and ecological change in India's central provinces 1860–1914*. New Delhi: Oxford University Press.

Rao, N. and Suresh, K. T. 2001. Domestic tourism in India. In Ghimire, K. (ed.) *The Native Tourist: Mass tourism within developing countries*. London: Earthscan.

Rathore, A. S., Prasad, H. and Jodhana, L. S. 2010. Financial performance of Rajasthan Tourism Development Corporation (RTDC): An analysis. *South Asian Journal of Tourism and Heritage* 3(1), 129–135.

Ravichandran, S. and Suresh, S. 2010. Using wellness services to position and promote Brand India. *International Journal of Hospitality & Tourism Administration* 11(2), 200–217.

Rediff.com. 2003. *Govt launches special tourism campaign for NRIs*. Available online: http://www.rediff.com//money/2003/jan/10pbd11.htm.

Reeve, J. and Edwards, V. 2002. *Visitor Codes in Indian Protected Areas: Worth the paper they are written on?* Paper presented at the Tourism and the Natural Environment International Conference, University of Brighton, October.

Richards, G. (ed.). 2001. *Cultural Attractions and European Tourism*. Wallingford: CABI.

Riley, P. J. 1988. Road culture of international long-term budget travellers. *Annals of Tourism Research* 15(3), 313–328.

Rojek, C. and Urry, J. (eds). 1997. *Touring Cultures: Transformations of travel and theory*. London: Routledge.

Rolfes, M. 2009. Poverty tourism: Theoretical reflections and empirical findings regarding an extraordinary form of tourism. *GeoJournal*. Available online: DOI 10.1007/s10708-009-9311-8.

Roy, A. 1997. *The God of Small Things*. London: Harper.

Ryan, C. and Saward, J. 2004. The zoo as ecotourism attraction – visitor reactions, perceptions and management implications: The case of Hamilton Zoo, New Zealand. *Journal of Sustainable Tourism* 12(3), 245–266.

Sagreiya, K. 1967. *Forests and Forestry*. New Delhi: National Book Trust.

Said, E. 1978. *Orientalism*. Harmondsworth: Penguin.

Saldanha, A. 2002. Music tourism and factions of bodies in Goa. *Tourist Studies* 2(1), 43–62.

Saldanha, A. 2005. Trance and visibility at dawn: Racial dynamics in Goa's rave scene. *Social & Cultural Geography* 6(5), 707–721.

Saldanha, A. 2007. *Psychedelic White: Goa, trance and the viscosity of race*. London: University of Minnesota Press.

Sallnow, M. 1981. Communitas reconsidered: The sociology of Andean pilgrimage. *Man* 16, 163–182.

Sanderson, G. 1878. *Thirteen Years among the Wild Beasts of India*. London: W. H. Allen.

Scheyvens, R. 2002. Backpacker tourism and Third World development. *Annals of Tourism Research* 29(1), 144–164.

Sekhar, N. 1998. Crop and livestock depredation caused by wild animals in protected areas: The case of Sariska Tiger Reserve Rajasthan, India. *Environmental Conservation* 25(2), 160–171.

Sekher, M. 2001. Organized participatory resource management: Insights from community forestry practices in India, *Forest Policy and Economics* 3, 137–154.

Selinger, E. and Outterson, K. 2009. *The Ethics of Poverty Tourism.* Boston University School of Law Working Paper No. 09-29. Boston: Boston University.

Sen, S. 2003. 3-day meet ends, NRIs expect better times ahead. *The Times of India,* 11 January.

Shackley, M. 1996. *Wildlife Tourism.* London: Routledge.

Shackley, M., (ed.). 1998. *Visitor Management: Case studies from World Heritage Sites.* Oxford: Butterworth-Heinemann.

Sharma, K. 2000. *Rediscovering Dharavi: Stories from Asia's largest slum.* New Delhi: Penguin.

Sharpley, R. and Sundaram, P. 2005. Tourism: A sacred journey? The case of ashram tourism, India. *International Journal of Tourism Research* 7(3), 161–171.

Sheller, M. and Urry, J. 2004. *Tourism Mobilities: Places to play, places in play.* London: Routledge.

Shenhav-Keller, S. 1993. The Israeli souvenir: Its text and context. *Annals of Tourism Research* 20, 182–196.

Shinde, K. 2007. Pilgrimage and the environment: Challenges in a pilgrimage centre. *Current Issues in Tourism* 10(4), 343–365.

Shurmer-Smith, P. and Hannam, K. 1994. *World's of Desire, Realm's of Power: A cultural geography.* London: Edward Arnold.

'Silver Hackle'. 1929. *Indian Jungle Lore and the Rifle: Being notes on shikar and wild animal life.* Calcutta: Thacker.

Singh, R. A. 2006. Pilgrimage in Hinduism: Historical context and modern perspectives. In Timothy, D. and Olsen, D. (eds) *Tourism, Religion and Spiritual Journeys.* London: Routledge.

Singh, S. 2001. Indian tourism: Policy, performance and pitfalls. In Harrison, D. (ed.) *Tourism and the Less Developed World.* London: CAB International.

Singh, S. 2004. Religion, heritage and travel: Case references from the Indian Himalayas. *Current Issues in Tourism* 7(1), 44–65.

Singh, S. 2005. Secular pilgrimages and sacred tourism in the Indian Himalayas. *Geojournal* 64(3), 215–223.

Singh, S. 2009a. *India.* London: Lonely Planet.

Singh, S. 2009b. Domestic tourism: Searching for an Asian perspective. In Singh, S. (ed.) *Domestic Tourism in Asia: Diversity and divergence.* London: Earthscan.

Sivaramakrishnan, K. 1999. *Modern Forests: Statemaking and environmental change in colonial Eastern India.* Stanford, CA: Stanford University Press.

Skaria, A. 1999. *Hybrid Histories: Forests, frontiers and wildness in Western India.* New Delhi: Oxford University Press.

Smith, A. D. 1991. *National Identity.* London: Penguin.

Smith, M. K. 2009. *Issues in Cultural Tourism Studies.* London: Routledge.

Smith, M. and Puczko, L. (eds). 2009. *Health and Wellness Tourism.* Oxford: Butterworth-Heinemann.

Snodgrass, J. G. 2007. Names, but no homes, of stone: Tourism, heritage and the play of memory in a Bhat funeral feast. In Henderson, C. and Weisgrau, M. (eds) *Raj Rhapsodies: Tourism, heritage and the seduction of history.* Aldershot: Ashgate.

Spear, P. 1970. The Mughal Mansabdari system. In Leach, E. and Mukerjee, S. (eds) *Elites of South Asia.* Cambridge: Cambridge University Press.

Sreekumar, T. and Parayil, G. 2002. Contentions and contradictions of tourism as development option: The case of Kerala, India. *Third World Quarterly* 23(3), 529–548.

Srivastava, L. 2005. Mobile phones and the evolution of social behavior. *Business and Information Technology* 24(2), 111–129.

Stanley, N. 2000. Souvenirs, ethics and aesthetics: Some contemporary dilemmas in the South Pacific. In Hitchcock, M. and Teague, K. (eds) *Souvenirs: The material culture of tourism.* Aldershot: Ashgate.

Stebbing, E. P. 1911. *Jungle By-Ways in India: Leaves from the note-book of a sportsman and a naturalist.* London: John Lane.

Stebbins, R. 2007. *Serious Leisure: A perspective for our time.* London: Transaction.

Stephenson, M. 2002. Travelling to the ancestral homelands: The aspirations and experiences of a UK Caribbean community. *Current Issues in Tourism* 5(5), 378–425.

Stone, P. 2006. A dark tourism spectrum: Towards a typology of death and macabre related tourist sites, attractions and exhibitions. *Tourism* 54(2), 145–160.

Sunder, N. 2000. Unpacking the 'joint' in joint forest management. In Doornbos, M., Saith, A. and White, B. (eds) *Forests: Nature, people, power.* Oxford: Blackwell.

Sutcliffe, W. 1997. *Are You Experienced?* New Delhi: Penguin.

Tesfahuney, M. 1998. Mobility, racism and geopolitics. *Political Geography* 17(5), 499–515.

*Thaindian News.* 2008. Singapore woos Indian tourists as desis turn globetrotters. Available online: http://www.thaindian.com/newsportal/sports/singapore-woos-indian-tourists-as-desis-turn-globetrotters_100102931.html

Thrift, N. 1997. The still point. In Pile, S. and Keith, M. (eds) *Geographies of Resistance.* London: Routledge.

Timothy, D. 2001. *Tourism and Political Boundaries.* London: Routledge.

Timothy, D. 2005. *Shopping Tourism, Retailing and Leisure.* Clevedon: Channel View.

Timothy, D. and Guelke, J. (eds). 2008. *Geography and Genealogy: Locating personal pasts.* London: Ashgate.

Tirumala, L. N. 2009. Bollywood movies and cultural identity construction amongst second-generation Indian Americans. Master's thesis, College of Mass Communications, Texas Tech University.

Tolia-Kelly, D. 2006. Mobility/stability: British Asian cultures of 'landscape and Englishness'. *Environment and Planning A* 38(2), 341–358.

Tourism Ireland. 2009. *Targeting Indian Tourists for Kilkenny.* Tourism Ireland press release, 6 April.

Travelblogs.com. 2009. *10 Reasons to Go Flashpacking the Next Time You Travel.* Available online: http://www.travelblogs.com/articles/10-reasons-to-go-flashpacking-the-next-time-you-travel

Tully, M. 1991. *No Full Stops in India.* London: Viking.

Tunbridge, J. E. and Ashworth, G. J. 1996. *Dissonant Heritage: The management of the past as a resource in conflict.* Chichester: John Wiley.

Turley, S. 2001. Children and the demand for recreational experiences: The case of zoos. *Leisure Studies* 20(1), 1–18.

Turner, V. and Turner, E. 1978. *Image and Pilgrimage in Christian Culture.* Oxford: Blackwell.

UNESCO. 1972. *UNESCO World Heritage Convention.* Available online: http://whc.unesco.org/en/conventiontext/

UNESCO. 2008a. *Operational Guidelines for the Implementation of the World Heritage Convention.* Paris: UNESCO.

UNESCO. 2008b. *Taj Mahal.* Available online: http://whc.unesco.org/en/list/252

Urry, J. 1990/2002. *The Tourist Gaze: Leisure and travel in contemporary societies.* London: Sage.

Urry, J. 2007. *Mobilities.* Cambridge: Polity Press.

Uy, D. 2007. Opening doors for Indian tourists. *Manila Standard Today*, 24 February. Available online: http://www.manilastandardtoday.com/2007/feb/24/goodLife1.htm

Van der Veer, P. 1995. Introduction: The diasporic imagination. In P. Van der Veer (ed.) *Nation and Migration: The politics of space in the South Asian diaspora*, Philadelphia: University of Pennsylvania Press.

Varma, P. 2004. *Being Indian.* London: Viking.

Vasudevan, R. 2003. Selves made strange: Violent and performative bodies in the cities of Indian cinema, 1974–2003. In Chandrasekhar, I. and Seel, P. (eds) *Body.City: Siting contemporary culture in India.* New Delhi: Tulika Books.

Vetcha, R. and Bhaskar, T. 2003. Passage . . . back to India. *The Hindu*, Sunday magazine supplement, 12 January.

Voice of Assam. 2010. *Voice of Assam: A digest with differing views.* Available online: http://www.voiceofassam.com/

Wadhwa, S. 2004. The hoax of 'God's Own Country'. *Outlook*, 12 July.

Walker, S. 2001. Zoological gardens of India. In Kisling, V. (ed.) *Zoo and Aquarium History.* London: CRC.

Washbrook, D. 1981. Law, state and agrarian society in colonial India. *Modern Asian Studies* 15(3), 649–721.

Watson, H. and Kopachevsky, J. 1994. Interpretations of tourism as commodity. *Annals of Tourism Research* 20, 643–660.

Wearing, S. 2001. *Volunteer Tourism: Experiences that make a difference.* Wallingford: CABI.

Wheeler, B. 1991. Tourism's troubled times: Responsible tourism is not the answer. *Tourism Management* 12(2), 91–96.

Williams, C. 2008. Ghettotourism and voyeurism, or challenging stereotypes and raising consciousness? Literary and non-literary forays into the favelas of Rio de Janeiro. *Bulletin of Latin American Research* 27(4), 483–500.

Williams, A. and Hall, C. M. 2002. Tourism, migration, circulation and mobility. In Hall, C. M. and Williams, A. (eds) *Tourism and Migration: New relationships between production and consumption.* Dordrecht: Kluwer.

Wilson, D. 1997. Paradoxes of tourism in Goa. *Annals of Tourism Research* 24(1), 52–75.

Young, R. 1995. *Colonial Desire: Hybridity in theory, culture, and race.* London: Routledge.

Young, Z., Makoni, G. and Boehmer-Christiansen, S. 2001. Green aid in India and Zimbabwe – conserving whose community? *Geoforum* 32, 299–318.

# Index